The Dweller Near A Pear Tree

Angela Busch

KELSO PRESS

KELSO PRESS

Waterman's End House
Matching Green
Essex CM17 0RQ

First published in 1996

ISBN 0-953 7633-0-7

Acknowledgements

I wish to express my sincerest thanks to all that helped to make this book a reality:

The Perry family and the Shimmen family for their help, support and loan of photographs. Patrick Streeter for his special interest, guidance, practical assistance and enormous encouragement. Gwyn Piff and Mike Ritchie for their kind help in early proof reading. Reverend Charles Masheder for the kind loan of the Parish records and for obtaining additional information for a family tree.

The Essex Records Office, the British Library and all local people who were kind enough to help in many different ways and for the kind loan of photographs, drawings and books. And especially to my husband, Axel Busch, for his unstinting support, great patience and magnificent editing skills.

To Fred Perry
- a very special friend

Ernest Williams, 26 South St, Bishop's Stortford.

Frederick John Perry - 1929

This story would most probably never have been written but for my getting to know Drammie. She was really named Lady McDram, but I have always called her just Drammie.

When she was born, I was already seventy-eight years old, but I can sincerely say that the age difference has never been a problem. In fact, it simply never came up -- Drammie and I understood each other from the word go.

Not that I had known her right from birth. You see, new people had moved into Waterman's End, the place I have known all my life.

Chapter 1

"I'll have him," Henry Lucking bellowed at the schoolmaster. Henry Lucking was the tenant farmer from Waterman's End and his massive frame, clad in a tweed coat, breeches and gaiters, towered over me as he spoke, his finger poised to tap me on the shoulder.

I, Frederick John Perry, was twelve years old and this, to my great sadness, was the end of my schooldays. The shortage of labour during the First World War had claimed me for work on the land at Waterman's End.

One day I sat on a school bench and the very next day I was a farm labourer. Henry Lucking made me work hard. I was employed as a labourer and he made me labour. But then, I had known that he would as I had known Mr Lucking for some years. After school, at weekends and during summer holidays, I had worked for him since I was nine years old. Chopping wood, polishing boots, carting coal, fetching paraffin and emptying rubbish pails. My reward for a Saturday and a Sunday was one shilling and sixpence.

Henry Lucking, my employer, was a great, big, jovial man. His bald head was invariably covered by a 'sugar pudding hat' -- a bit like a trilby hat but floppier -- and he was never seen without his pipe.

He was a mean-fisted tyrant to work for, but was always ready for some fun. His face was forever beaming with laughter.

Often he would wave his hat in the air and sing a little limerick he had just made up on the spur of the moment. All his farm hands knew exactly what was in store for them when he rode into the farm yard each morning, the bicycle frame groaning under his weight. A big grin on his face indicated that he had a funny story or somebody's misdemeanour to regale, whilst a stern face indicated a severe scolding, or worse, for somebody.

Now, in 1917, when I was twelve years old, Henry Lucking employed me as a farm labourer at three shillings and sixpence a week. To protest at having been removed from school or at becoming a farm labourer would never have occurred to me. It would have been unthinkable. After all, we children all knew what was expected of us. There was a war on and we were fighting that nasty man, the Kaiser, with his huge waxed moustache. We had all seen what real soldiers looked like and much of our time was spent playing soldiers. With a wooden stick held against our shoulder like a gun, we marched stiff-legged across our village green chanting rhymes about the Kaiser:

> *"I shan't go to heaven,*
> *I know very well,*
> *but it is really too bad*
> *to be kicked out of hell."*

We children would all gladly have joined up if the army would have taken us. But, instead, we were claimed for the land.

On my first working day, I carted sheaves of wheat across Mill Hill Field at Waterman's End Farm. The supply of wheat seemed inexhaustible and the field huge. I thought that the task would never be finished -- or surely not before my arms and legs gave out. This was a devastating change from having enjoyed sitting on the school bench and listening to the cultured voice of the schoolmaster.

After what seemed an eternity, lunch time arrived. Completely shattered by the unaccustomed heavy work, I sank to the ground, leaned against a gatepost and unpacked my bread and cheese.

The crusty old horsekeeper was sitting close by and observed me from under his bushy eyebrows. He was determined that the new boy should make his own life easier and before I even had a chance to take my first bite, he ordered: "Put that nosebag on the horse."

I timidly took the nosebag and tried to put it on the carthorse. As my little arms reached up to fit the strap over the huge horse's head, the animal flung its head up, hit me under the chin and knocked me flying straight into the field. I winced, got up and tried to gather my wits.

The horsekeeper drew his breath in sharply, and slowly got to his feet. He glowered at me, grabbed my arm and whacked me sharply round the ear with his cap. He was absolutely furious with me for having 'wasted' the horse's feed. This was a serious problem as grain for the horses was doled out to the horsekeeper on a weekly basis. The grain store was unlocked, each day's feed was carefully measured out, and now he was short a meal.

After a few days, I was given the task of looking after a herd of young cattle. If a crop grew too early and 'raced away', the cattle were put into the field so they could eat the tops to slow down the growth. It was hot and hard work to run up and down the field trying to prevent the cattle from disappearing through one of the many holes in the hedge.

A dozen or more cows were quite hard to handle for a young lad, but, out of sheer necessity, I learned fast.

One of the larger holes I covered with my button-down

jersey. I was so hot and bothered from rushing around that I had no need for it anyhow. One especially obstinate -- or plain stupid -- cow, however, still had her mind firmly set on getting through that hole. She stuck her horns right through my jersey -- one sleeve on each horn.

Now unable to see where she was going, she was bumping into other cows and generally creating havoc while I was in hot pursuit. Eventually, with the help of a fork handle, I succeeded in recovering my precious garment, which was none the worse for the experience.

But my early working days were very much overshadowed by my unhappiness over my need to leave school. I had enjoyed my last few years at school.

While in the first few years it had been a chore, now learning had become fun. I had been looking forward to more of it. I had taken great pride in improving my marks and seeing ticks against my schoolwork rather than crosses. I had become quite good at it, even presumptuously thought myself a little brighter than my classmates - - and now it was all over.

I was born in 1905 at Perry Cottage, Matching Green. My father was in the army and my mother returned to 'being in service' shortly after my birth. I grew up with my grandparents at Perry Cottage. Granny had brought up her own thirteen children on her husband's pay of eleven shillings a week, or twenty-eight pounds a year. Only her youngest son, Jimmy, still lived at home. The other children were either married or the younger girls in service.

Matching Green School - 1913
(in the Parish of High Laver)

Front row: (left to right) 1 Ginny Clarke, 2 Ethel Clarke, 3 Edith Clark, 4 May Clark,
5 Dulcie Whitbread, 6 Hettie Whitbread, 7 Violet Barker, 8 May Peacock

Second row: (left to right) 1 Winnie Patmore, 2 unknown, 3 George Blowes, 4 Harry
Whitbread, 5 Jim Holgate, 6 Chris Whitbread, 7 Joe Holgate, 8 Jim Peacock,
9 Leslie Blackmore

Third row: (left to right) 1 unknown, 2 Dolly Houchin, 3 Lily Peacock, 4 Mary Wren,
5 Mary Perry, 6 Winnie Byford, 7 Olive Holgate, 8 Marjory Bass, 9 Irene Smith,
10 Lydia Smith

Fourth row: (left to right) 1 Mrs Bentley, 2 Mr Bentley, 3 Fred Walden, 4 unknown,
5 Harry Trundle, 6 Sam Whitbread, 7 Bertie Lyon, 8 David Whitbread,
9 Johnny Holgate, 10 Len Peacock, 11 Will collins, 12 Charlie Collins, 13 Miss Emily Brown

Back row: (left to right) 1 Alfie Branch, 2 Albert Houchin, 3 Johnny Perrin,
4 **Frederick John Perry**, 5 Fred Perry, 6 Victor Bartrum, 7 Jack Collins

The hard life of the very poor had toughened Granny, and to others she appeared somewhat formidable. She was small and stout in stature; her long, black skirts swished across the bare floor of our cottage. When Granny was angry, God help us. She would stand, feet splayed, lips tight and brow wrinkled; her arms folded across her chest, which made them look like great, big vegetable marrows to my child's eyes. I learned quickly not to cross Granny or to fall foul of her opinion as to how a young lad should behave 'properly'.

'Granny'
Sarah Ann Perry, 1851 - 1936

"I ent havin' none o' that," she would say lifting her hand threateningly if she thought that I might be up to some mischief. "Ya ma'k ma words. I'll larn ya."

Granny spoke with the typical Essex accent of our area. The various dialects varied markedly from one rural Essex area to another. We always knew if there was a 'foreigner' about who might come from a village only six or eight miles away. Unfortunately these lovely local Essex voices have been lost over the years. There are only a few old people left who speak in the dialect of my childhood.

Granny was fifty-four years old when I was born, but to my child's eyes she always looked terribly old. Like with all the old women, one could only have guessed at their shape. They were swaddled in layers and layers of clothes. Granny always wore voluminous dark floor-length shirts from under which the toe-caps of her stout hobnailed boots would peep out. Her dark blouse or top garment she always referred to as her 'body'. The clothes were never new. I have never known Granny to have a new skirt or dress. She could not have afforded it. All her clothes were hand-me-downs or second hand bought at a rummage sale.

Her pride and joy though was her white apron. The apron would be put on in the afternoon whenever somebody important called. Not neighbours or locals, but possibly if the rector was due to visit. Otherwise the apron was only worn on Sundays. Granny considered herself smartly dressed only when she had her clean white apron on.

Granny was a wonderful cook. Considering that she had very little to put in her pots, I recall that I loved her food. She had a way of making very little taste special.

Yet most days started on a meagre ration. "Tea kettle broth this morning, met," Granny would say to me. This was some hot water, a crust or two of bread, a bit of butter or margarine floating on top and salt and pepper for taste. On rare occasions, when I had fetched enough water from the village pump to neighbours' houses and had earned an extra tuppence, we were able to get a little more milk. On such feast days, Granny would make me my special favourite: milk mess. This was bread soaked in milk.

Clothes, for adults and children alike, were generally supplied by Mr Carruthers, a travelling man. Weekly, he would arrive in a smart pony trap which bulged with clothing he had brought from his big shop, 'Bon Marche', in the nearby county town of Bishops Stortford. He was a most benevolent man and helped the poor of the village a great deal. We were able to acquire new or secondhand clothing from him and pay as, and when, we could: a sixpence one week and only a penny the next.

"I wonder if you have an old jacket that might fit my boy?" Granny inquired on one occasion, pointing at me. "I can't afford to buy him one, sir."

"I'll see what I can do Mrs Perry," Mr Carruthers replied.

Sure enough, next week kind Mr Carruthers arrived with a 'Beetle Tail' jacket for me: three buttons at the back and a sparrow's tail -- just as they are worn at weddings. Whilst Granny was delighted to have a warm jacket for me, I eyed it with rather mixed feelings. It didn't bother me particularly that when I wore it at school I became the laughing stock of my mates. What I did mind very much, however, was playing in it after school. I spotted my own shadow -- and lo and behold I looked exactly like a cock pheasant.

That was that! My seven year old dignity was deeply injured. I was not going to look like a pheasant, and so flatly refused to wear the jacket again. After many tantrums, much screeching and bellyaching, Granny finally gave in. She took the offending article to the post office shop and exchanged it for a bundle of bacon bones.

Good riddance -- and we tucked in to a wonderful bacon stew that evening!

Granny constantly had to worry about suitable clothes for me and I had, yet again, worn out one of my shoes. Oh dear, it was very painful to walk in the shoe in its sorry state, split all the way round so that it looked like a fish with its mouth open.

Grandpa Holgate, the next door neighbour, a small, wizened man sporting a permanent fuzzy beard, thought he could help.

"I think you'll find an old'un in the shed," he said. To Granny's and my delight, we did indeed find an old 'heavy decker shoe'. Even though we called it a shoe, it was in fact a hobnailed working boot. Shoes were lightweight boots worn only on Sundays by the better-off villagers and I didn't get a pair until I was quite grown up and had earned the money myself.

This boot was black, had steel caps at the toe and heel, a hobnailed sole and laced up to just above the ankle. Just what was needed. Granny stuck the stove brush up our chimney and polished the shoe with soot. "There you go," she said "That'll match your other one just fine." But, my foot could just slip right out of the big, heavy 'new' shoe. "Never mind," Granny exclaimed. "You'll have to make do and you'll grow into it soon enough."

Next morning, on our way to school, my friends and I played our usual hurdle game. We pushed two rough sticks into the ground and placed another one across the top. Then we jumped over. As soon as we had mastered this height, the top stick was raised a notch. On this occasion, my friend and neighbour Jack Holgate jumped first. He cleared the hurdle. I would have to match that. I jumped. I can't remember if I actually cleared the top stick, but my 'new' shoe certainly did. It sailed over and landed some distance down the road.

I had no brothers or sisters, much to my regret but undoubtedly to Granny's delight. I had to look for company to the house next door where the Holgates and the Whitbreads lived. Each family had a brood of thirteen children and I was not short of companionship.

One of my favourites amongst the neighbours' children was Siberetta Whitbread. She looked after me like an older sister; always ready to lend a sympathetic ear or smooth my ruffled feathers. On how Siberetta got her name, I do not wish to speculate, but I am sure the Whitbreads could not possibly have known even how to spell Siberetta. The schoolmaster called her Siberetta and we accepted that; even if it was a rather grand sounding name for a girl who would never have had a clean frock unless she had washed it herself.

Christmas was a favourite time for us children. I hung my stocking up each year not expecting very much. My expectations always proved right -- empty. Yet, after I had nagged her persistently, Granny prepared a Christmas tree for me one year. She took a cactus off the window sill and stuck a few sugar mice on the cactus spikes. I was very proud indeed but somewhat less pleased when I saw my pet rabbit lying on the kitchen table, ready to be skinned. For months I had carefully collected delectable greens for him. Dandelion leaves had been his favourite food and now my playmate was going to be our Christmas lunch.

The biggest treat of all on Christmas Day was going to church and chapel, where we were given a piece of real plum cake -- my only chance to taste such a delicacy.

The great day had arrived and Siberetta stuck her head through our door and called out to me: "All right, Perry, I'll take you to chapel."

"You can't take him," Granny retorted: "I haven't finished his trousers yet."

"Never mind," Siberetta answered, looking at Granny's handiwork. "They'll do. We are only walking just across the Green to chapel."

Granny hastily put in a few more stitches while I brushed my hair, spat on a flannel and rubbed it round my face. Siberetta took my hand and we set off, crossing the village green together with quite a brood of Whitbread and Holgate children. When we reached the cricket ground in the middle of the Green, we all decided to jump the cricket chains.

Under Siberetta's watchful eye I jumped over and landed safely on the other side. Clucking over me like a mother hen, Siberetta decided that I did not look very spruce, which indeed I didn't. "Look at all those bits of cotton hanging down," she said and tugged at the loose threads -- off came my trousers, in three bits. I never made it to chapel on that particular Christmas Day. But, bless Siberetta, she still brought me back my piece of plum cake.

I often hear people speak in sentimental tones of the 'good ol' days'. Were they 'good'? I am not so sure. They were the days we knew best, of course, and I certainly think back with great fondness to those times. But sometimes I think that they weren't so good, certainly not for the likes of Granny. They were blooming tough and we were very poor. But this didn't bother us children very much at all. In the carefree spirit of youth, we didn't mind one bit. They were wonderfully happy days for us. So much hardship is hard to understand if you have been brought up in more recent times, but at the time, we children didn't know any different. That was our world.

Sometimes there were feast days even in the Perry household, as on the occasion when a pair of ducks were foolish enough to waddle from a neighbouring farm into our back meadow. Grandfather was a very gentle man and I saw him hesitate for a few moments. Then 'needs must' took over. Well, this was too much to ask even from an honest man like Grandfather. He lifted the long-handled hoe he had been using on his vegetable beds and hit the ducks over the head.

"Those bu'rds (birds) were in our garden. Those bu'rds are ours."

The news that the policeman, who lived just across the Green, had been asked to investigate, reached us like greased lightning.

The constable went from house to house in his search. With his helmet under his arm he ducked his head and stepped through the doorway into our house.

"Search the house. You'll find nothing here," Granny said, shrugging her shoulders while vigorously kneading some dough on the table.

The police constable had a voice which sounded like someone tearing a sack, and after having had a good look around the house, he rasped: "There is certainly nothing here." He left closing the door behind himself.

As my stomach slowly unknotted I whispered to Granny: "Where are they?"

"They are sitting very close to my arse," she retorted.

Enterprising Granny had put a piece of string across her shoulders, tied a duck to each end and had tucked them into her wide-legged drawers, well hidden under her voluminous long skirts.

"I knew he wouldn't lay a hand on me," she chuckled.

One has to remember that my grandparents were of a generation that would take such a risk out of the sheer need to feed us and at considerable peril to themselves. Offence against property was a very serious crime and hunger positively not a defence. If grandfather had been caught and convicted for stealing two ducks -- even if they were in our garden -- the sentence would more than likely have been three months hard labour.

My grandparents also still remembered the locals they had known who had been transported to lands beyond the seas for what we now consider as such minor crimes as poaching. Grandfather told me how he had walked all the way to Chelmsford to see a man hang for stealing sheep. I believe he didn't see the hanging, for he fainted first.

English law in those days was bristling with capital felonies. It seems to me that English law was written in blood. Where is this great British justice I hear about? Recent accounts of miscarriages of justice, so well publicised by all the media, make me think that not very much has changed. It appears to me that today, as at the beginning of the century, if you have the right connections and can afford a good lawyer you may benefit from the great British justice. If not, you seem to be little better off than at the beginning of the century.

My only consolation is that we English may still be more civilised than most. I read somewhere that France did not abolish transportation until 1938. Even then they did not let the poor blighters go free. Whoever had been previously transported was still detained. Well, we have all heard of Devil's Island just off the coast of French Guyana, which was not abandoned until sometime during the Second World War.

Obtaining food, however, to fill our hungry bellies was not always as easy as bu'rds wandering into our garden. As soon as we children could walk well enough, we had to help 'gleaning'.

After harvest, as soon as the removal of the sheaves of wheat from the fields was completed, the village women were allowed to glean the fields, which meant they had permission to take the bits of corn left behind.

During the next few weeks, the women moved up and down the fields. Backs aching from the continuous bending, their long skirts always catching on the stubble, the women, helped by their children, picked up each and every ear of corn from the ground. Whenever more ears had been gathered than could comfortably be held in one hand, they were tied into little bundles like bouquets. Short ears and individual grains were put into the short ear bag. It was back-breaking work but the women knew that the corn would be essential in helping them to feed their families. It was a tedious and tiring task for anybody, but particularly for a bored, hungry little chap like me. I hated gleaning.

"I am hungry Granny."

"Well, little met," Granny said, patting my head, "see that clock over there on Little Laver Hall stables -- Park Clock? Ya may have yar bit of victuals when the clock strikes twelve...and nit 'fore."

Each evening, we took our gleaned corn back to Perry Cottage. If at the end of gleaning we had managed to collect a bushel, Granny would be very pleased. But you had to collect an awful lot of ears to make up a bushel and we did not manage it very often. To protect the corn from vermin, we stored it in our big wooden kneading trough. Nobody wanted to take the slightest chance of mice or sparrows sharing in our painstakingly gathered grain.

Some time later, the threshing machine would come to the local farms to thresh their corn. And whenever the farmer had knocked off work at the end of the day, the villagers arrived to have their small quantity of corn threshed for a few pence.

Thereafter, it only remained to carry the corn for grinding at Little Laver Mill about a mile and a half down the lane. Finally, the finished flour was carried back home and put in a bin where it was safely stored until baking day

Little Laver Mill
Leaves from a Hunting Diary in Essex, by H Beauchamp Yerburgh, 1900

Just outside Perry Cottage stood a nice, brick-built bakehouse erected by the landlord many years before for the use of all his cottagers. The women would light the baking ovens very early on baking day. Faggots were ideal for baking, so the women said. Coal, they claimed, somehow did not produce the right kind of heat. The women all got together and helped each other to prepare and bake the lovely crusty bread which we relished so much. When the smell of fresh bread filled the air, we children were never very far away .

15

Chapter 2

Our village of Matching Green is in the lovely countryside of West Essex about eight miles from the market town of Bishops Stortford. Matching is an old village, its origins dating back to Saxon times. In the Domesday Book of 1086 it is called by its Saxon name -- Matcinga.

Matching Green
Leaves from a Hunting Diary in Essex, by H Beauchamp Yerburgh, 1900

The village green was, and still is today, a triangular common with each leg of the triangle about 250 yards long, with the cricket ground right in the middle. Early this century, in my early childhood, two farms, a few substantial houses, several shops and about three dozen cottages were dotted along the edge of the Green.

The village of Matching Green had very good facilities. There were the two pubs -- the Chequers, and the Cherry Tree which was the smarter of the two. The Chequers also had an

16

adjacent butcher's shop, a coal yard, livery stables and a pony trap hire service.

The Taylor family at Albion House ran the biggest of the village stores, the draper's and grocer's shop with an adjoining bakery.

The post office shop was a general store run by the Owers family and there was another shop just off the Green on the High Laver Road called Curry's, which sold books, newspapers and all sorts of general goods.

In addition, there was Silcock's, the saddlers and bootmakers, where farmers met for their tattle. John Saville, the blacksmith at the forge, also carried out any wheelwright's work. But most popular of all with us children was Willie Walden's bicycle shop. We lingered at his shop a lot, if he didn't chase us away. There were all sorts of things which could usefully be converted into superb toys. For a penny, Willie Walden would take out the spokes from an old, redundant bicycle wheel and this made the best of all hoops. Such a hoop was a prized possession.

Mr Wortley ran the main butcher's shop. Another was attached to the Chequers pub.

There was no shortage of places where you could spend your money which, of course, the cottagers had little of. Some of the shopkeepers were quite sympathetic to their needs and would give credit until the next few pence or shillings came in. The post office shop helped Granny out on many occasions. But they knew their customers well. Nothing was much of a secret on the Green, and those who 'would not fritter away their hard-earned shillings on paying their debts', were never allowed tick.

In addition to our own shops, many travelling merchants came to the Green in their brightly painted horse-drawn vans with the name of their firms displayed on the sides of the vehicles. Three butchers' box carts called and two millers' came and offered their wares of poultry seeds, grains, fertiliser and bags of flour. Basket women would walk from door to door trying to sell anything from pins to brushes and pots and pans. The milk round consisted of a pony trap carrying milk churns full of skimmed milk. But the better-off villagers would mostly buy their milk from the local farms as this 'new' milk was much creamier and made a lovely rice pudding.

Two fishmongers, several tailors and many grocers' vans came and sold their goods on the Green. A haberdasher arrived once a week. Even the big Harlow store of Jacobs and Archibalds sent a van over. If you had the money, you could order anything.

On the other hand, many women did not know how to make ends meet and I am quite sure that some of them settled their debts by going upstairs with the merchants. In fact, it was common knowledge that the farmer from Elms farm would walk into the field where the women were working and openly offer a two shilling piece to whoever would disappear behind the hedge with him.

"Which one today?" he would ask holding the coin up between finger and thumb. And many of the old women did go. He paid them eighteen pence for a hard day's work and two shillings for a few minutes behind the hedge.

Several times a week the horse of a 'Cheap Jack' would pull onto the Green. These tradesmen came in a specially fitted open van -- exactly like a big dresser on wheels. The shelves were stacked with plates and various items of china and earthenware. Dangling from hooks were cups, jugs, chamber pots, cooking pots and pans. On the back hung a selection of tin baths.

They were called 'Cheap Jacks' because they were always a couple of pennies cheaper than a shop. The goods were often a little chipped or damaged, but that did not worry the buyers.

We children would especially look forward to the arrival of the windmill man who came twice a year. He would exchange jam or pickling jars for paper windmills. How many jars you could give him dictated the size of the windmill you would receive. The villagers could not afford to buy toys, but occasionally they could spare a jar or two for a windmill for us.

Jars were a treasured commodity. The fish man would also exchange them: two jars for two herrings or a bloater. Or you might exchange a rabbit skin, or some mole skins for some fish or a couple of oranges, which were also sold from the fish van. A good clean rabbit skin would fetch sixpence. A fox fur was rarer, but a very valuable item. It would fetch one pound.

The fishmonger's cart featured a long tailboard at the back, which extended almost to the ground. Underneath the tailboard hung the rabbit and mole skins, while boxes of fish, packed in ice, sat on the top of the board.

The Green was a very active place indeed, particularly during the summer, when it was as busy as a beehive. All houses faced on to the Green and to go anywhere -- to work, shops or school -- you had to walk along it or cross it, always well observed by the neighbours.

It was also bustling with animals, dotted with little hen coops, which is possibly too grand a description for what were essentially just wooden sugar boxes laid on their side to provide some shelter with some wire strung around them. The hens, chicks, ducks and goslings stayed on the Green all summer long.

Only a very few houses had their own meadows and therefore most horses were turned out on to the Green. The post office had three ponies, the blacksmith had one, at the Chequers pub there were six to eight liveried horses, while Spencer, the haycarter, kept three or four. In fact, every tradesman plus anybody else who kept a horse, grazed them on the Green during the summer. There must have been thirty horses.

Out of sheer mischief, we boys would sometimes take a couple of them and lead them up Watery Lane towards Waterman's End. It always amused us that as soon as we let go of them, they would just turn right around and walk straight back to the Green. They could have stopped at any point to graze on a grass verge, but no, they would trot straight back. They liked the Green better. I can only assume that the various wild herbs which grew amongst the grasses made grazing there more delicious. There was white clover, sanfoine, trefoil, lucerne, dari, wild millet and many pretty little wild flowers, which were also much loved by bees, birds and butterflies.

All houses had gates to prevent livestock wandering into the vital and therefore well-guarded vegetable gardens.

Occasionally, when a farmer needed his meadow for hay, he also would send his cows on to the Green, but that was not very popular as nobody wanted these heavy cloven-footed beasts near the fine lawn of the cricket grounds; the other reason being that whilst horse manure was quite easy to gather up and useful as a fertiliser, cow pats were a different proposition.   They were not at all easy to pick up.

For short periods, we would sometimes have sheep with a shepherd in attendance.

In the spring, however, all sheep were brought on to the Green for dipping. The farmers would get together and help each other. There was a special dipping pond on the Green. Into this pond the sheep dip would be poured and a shallow channel cut across the Green to the main pond.

The sheep were then driven into the dipping ponds, out the other side, along the channel and into the big ponds. A lot of very soggy sheep would emerge from the pond by the post office.

Also, whoever could afford to do so, kept a flock of geese on the Green.

Women regularly interrupted their indoor tasks to walk on to the Green to feed their poultry, whilst perhaps also having a chat or a gossip with their neighbours. All water had to be carried home from the three pumps on the Green. None of the cottages had their own water pump and every drop had to be fetched. Carrying water to neighbouring houses was how we youngsters were often able to earn an extra penny.

Our nearest pump was at the Chequers, about 200 yards from Perry Cottage. Some of the villagers obtained their washing water from the four ponds on the Green, but we were lucky in having a deep water-filled ditch running along the perimeter of the garden at the back of Perry Cottage and our washing water came from there.

We might even have had the luxury of mains water had not the Parish Council in their wisdom - or tightfistedness -- in 1907 decided that it was 'not needed.'

Meeting of the Parish Council held in the Schoolroom on March 27th 1907

Present Mess. J. J. Howard, W. H. Hawkins C. E. Pollard & C. Clark.

The minutes of last meeting were read, passed & signed.

Proposed by Mr. Hawkins seconded by Mr. Pollard that a precept be issued on the Overseers for £1. 3. 6 & that the following bills be paid vis

Boardman	6. 3
Harper	5. 8
Postage	1. 6

Carried

A letter from the Herts & Essex Water Co. proposing to extend their water main to Matching Green was considered, also one from the Epping Rural District Council asking for the Parochial Committees report on the matter

Proposed by Mr. Hawkins seconded by Mr. Pollard "that this Parochial Committie having considered the matter are of the opinion that the water main is not needed, as there is a good supply of water both at Matching Tye & Matching Green & there is no likelehood of being any return for the outlay & they would also point out that two-thirds of the houses on Matching Green are in High Laver parish.   Carried Unanimously.

Minutes from Matching Parish Council - 27.3.1907

The Green was, of course, also the playground for dozens of children. They were shunted outside to play as soon as they could toddle. There certainly wasn't room enough for them in the cottages while their mothers were trying to get on with their tasks.

The cottagers often had large families and the houses were far too small to accommodate them. On either side of us at Perry Cottage our neighbours, the Whitbreads and the Holgates, had thirteen children each. How did they fit such a large family into a small house with two tiny bedrooms? The answer is with great difficulty, and at night the calico covered straw mattresses had to be laid out very carefully to give everybody a sleeping space.

Mind you, the thirteen children would never be at home all at once at any one time. Some children did not survive to their teens and by the time the youngest was born, several of the older ones would have left home already. Without fail, girls left home at the age of twelve or thirteen. They went into service or 'sa'vice' as the locals called it.

Just as the farmers came to school and chose us boys, employers would also come to school and pick the girls off the school bench. Provided they were known as good employers, the parents would be delighted at their daughters being chosen as it meant one less mouth to feed. It was not that they did not care, or wanted to get rid of their children, it was just that all their energies had to go into keeping everybody fed and clothed, and a bit of extra space in the house would be needed as there was most probably another child on its way.

Mostly the girls would be delighted too. Like all youngsters, they could not wait to grow up. And they would be given clean uniforms: a nice print dress for mornings and a black dress for the afternoons. In addition, they wore beautifully starched and pressed white aprons and a white cap.

The girls looked very smart indeed. Never previously had they worn such lovely clothes, nor for that matter had they ever had a bed to themselves.

At first, the girls might take a position with a local farmer or at one of the larger houses in and around Matching Green. They all kept a few maids. Here these little maids would be well trained and, on the whole, well treated. The food was more plentiful and nourishing than the meagre rations at home which had needed to be shared with the other siblings.

A prime position for a young maid would be in the rectory because the rector knew so much more about the dire circumstances of the cottagers' lives, having visited their houses, and he might just provide a little extra for the young housemaid. He might pay to get her a pair of shoes to wear. Whilst uniforms were supplied by the employer, the maids generally had to supply their own shoes, which was not always easy for a young girl starting out in working life. The parents might very well not have enough money to send her off with a decent pair of shoes. But again, the tradesmen on the Green would often come to the rescue. Silcock's would provide the shoes on tick and the new wage earner would pay it off gradually. Half a crown paid off over a few months would buy her a wonderful pair of shoes.

The maids had one afternoon a week off, and provided it was not too far, they came home to visit their families. But often, by the time they had walked several miles home, there was little time left before they had to turn around for the walk back to their master's house.

These first jobs were important as the first rung on the career ladder in service. "That'll see her up the road," mothers said, meaning that once the girls were trained, they could go further afield and earn better money. Wages locally weren't much. I recall that my friend Peter Peacock's wife worked at Hull Green Farm for four shillings a month. This must have been in about 1915. Oh dear, how time has flown! It was Peter Peacock's grandfather who walked the countryside together with my Grandpa exercising their trade as thatchers -- and this year Peter will be celebrating his one hundredth birthday.

Once the young housemaids were trained and could slightly better their positions, they might work in a big house closer to London, while some even made it to London. Mothers sent their daughters to London with severe warnings ringing in their ears. They would have to be extremely careful in the big city. London, after all, was full of lads trying to take advantage of village girls.

In London the girls could earn eight shillings a month or more. At this point in their working lives, the girls generally returned home only once a year for their week or fortnight's holiday. Even if time had been long enough on an occasional day off to come home, the train fare would have been too exorbitant.

Girls had no options but to go into service. As long as they stayed at home, they could not earn any money. Boys, on the other hand, were not encouraged to leave home. Somehow, by hook or by crook, a sleeping space was found for them in the overcrowded houses. After all, as soon as they were old enough to work on the land, they would bring in a few shillings to help with the family expenses. This was the only way the cottagers could support their plentitude of children.

Whenever daughters came home for their annual vacation, sleeping arrangements in the cottages would be re-planned. All the girls might sleep with mother in the parents' room and father would sleep with the boys.

Compared with that of most of my childhood friends, the accommodation at Perry Cottage was spacious. During my early childhood, the cottage was occupied only by Granny, Grandpa, Uncle Jimmy and me -- plus the occasional daughter home from service. Granny would often allow one of the neighbouring children to sleep at our house to help ease the congestion in theirs. We, however, had to suffer the same plight as all our neighbours.

Fleas were a constant bane in our lives. Granny regularly ran the flame of a candle along my rough calico bed sheets where the fleas were known to be waiting for their human supper to go to bed. The heat of the flame would kill them off and give me some overnight respite from the little blighters. The fleas were not just a problem in the cottages. They were not fussy about social classes. Everybody suffered them. I can recall even the local squire coming home itching and saying: "I am going to have a bath. Picked up some fleas." Fleas were a fact of life.

At school our heads were regularly inspected for lice. If any child was badly affected by headlice, they were given some pomade to put on the hair and was sent home with instructions to wash the hair in carbolic soap before going to bed. For the next few days we children would invariably ostracise and tease the unfortunate schoolmate who had been sent home with lice. One little boy in addition to having suffered head lice was told off by the schoolmaster for coming to school with a very grubby face. Brown sticky molasses and bread crumbs were generously smeared right round his mouth.

"You have not washed your face this morning," the schoolmaster reprimanded little Joe.

"How could I?" the poor child replied. "My flannel was freez [frozen]."

Like most children, Joe came from a large family and as there was limited space in the house, ablutions were usually made outside. At Joe's house an old table was placed outside, a few rusty nails knocked into the legs as hangers for the bit a rag which doubled as a washing flannel.

The schoolmaster ordered one of the bigger girls to go along with little Joe to the boy's porch. There stood the washing basin and carbolic soap which we boys tried so very carefully to avoid. But on this occasion the girl supervised Joe's cleaning efforts.

"All right Joe, you lead us in this mornings' Lord's prayer," the schoolmaster said as a clean-faced Joe returned to the schoolroom.

"Our Father," the schoolmaster started him off.

"Works on t' farm at Waterman's End," Joe continued. -- This is how far Joe had got in learning 'Our Lord's Prayer'.

Granny always checked my face before I left for school.

"Come here!" Let me wipe yar fearce [face]," she pulled me over to her and if there was no water within easy reach, spat on a flannel and wiped it round my face - not so much a question of hygiene, more a matter of pride.

Fortunately I never suffered the humiliation of being sent home from school with lice as Granny was extremely fussy with what she called the louse trap, a very fine comb designed to catch any louse which might have jumped on your hair. These combs were euphemistically know as a 'small toothed comb' and available in every shop. Granny also forbade me to visit some houses which not only had flees and lice but also house-lice, e.g. bedbugs.

"Wh're you going?" Granny demanded to know as I was leaving the house.

"Yar not going there," she countermanded my reply. "I saw she in t'shop t'other day. She got red bugs [bedbugs] in t' housen."

Granny was very careful not to get any of these infestations in the house as these bloodsucking parasites were a real menace. Once established in a house, they were devilishly difficult to eradicate. Her theory was that swallows brought the bedbugs. There seemed to be an amazing coincidence between houses which had bugs and house swallows. I have never been able to establish if her theory holds water, but we certainly never had any swallows in our cottage.

I was also not allowed to visit a house which stood not far across our back meadow. Everybody called it 'Louse Hall'.

"Ya don't want to mix with they," Granny commanded "Ya can smell their fit (feet) from here.

A very rough, dirty farm labourer and his family lived there. When his bedpost broke, he replaced it with willow branch just pushed into the bare earth floor. As willow cuttings easily do in damp soil, this willow bedpost rooted and sprouted leaves. The father found it most convenient as now he not only had a new bedpost but also some branches to hang his clothes on. In 1912 one of the children accidentally knocked a lit paraffin lamp over and it burst into flames. Rather than dousing the fire, the family took fright and ran outside. The thatched roof of Louse Hall caught fire quickly and the house burned to the ground. I reckoned that was the only way that particular house could be rid of its bugs.

London bugs, however, were by far the worst. They were about the size of a ladybird, almost impossible to get rid of and were reputed to have been brought from London by the haycarters. London bugs would get into the cracks of the tattered old wallpaper in the cottages and lurk behind the paper until ready to strike at night. These bugs gave a particularly nasty bite. If somebody wanted to eliminate London bugs, the entire house had to be cleared, stripped and re-papered. Again, due to Granny's vigilance we never suffered that plaque.

As you can see, even in our very poor environment there were class distinctions. There was always a class below. There were people we looked down on because they were not clean or were riddled with bugs. Even the rector or doctor would only enter some houses if absolutely necessary and only after having tied up their trouser legs at the ankle to prevent bugs from crawling up their legs. Undoubtedly these poor, flee riddled families looked down on the people who had no house at all - - the labourers who lived in the farmer's barn, or the people in the workhouse or in poorhouses. And indeed, everybody looked down on the 'didicoys', the grubby travelling tinkers who pretended to be real gypsies. They were often light-fingered and lived on their wits. The proud genuine gypsies despised these pretenders.

Saturday was the cleaning day in most houses. It was a thoroughly uncomfortable time for us children. Very small children were sent on to the Green, no matter what the weather, because mothers wanted to get them out from under their feet, and slightly older ones would try to get out of the house as soon as possible in case they were commandeered to help.

Granny, however, while immensely careful over parasites and pests, did not take general cleaning too seriously. Just the very basic tasks were undertaken, though she was most fussy about keeping the chimney clean. She was very concerned about the thatched roof of Perry Cottage catching fire.

"Go cut me a branch," she would say, and either Grandfather or Uncle Jimmy would cut a branch out of the hedge, climb on to the roof and drop it down the chimney on a rope. The branch was then vigorously moved up and down, until all the soot was swept down into the fireplace -- and evenly deposited all over us and the house.

Most other major cleaning tasks would wait until one of her daughters came home from sa'vice for her annual holiday, and Granny would give her the task of giving Perry Cottage a good going over. I am sure they were pleased to go back to work after their 'vacation'.

My Aunt Jessie was the one to whom this task fell most often. But on this day she had taken a little time out to build a swing for me in our shed. She slung two ropes over the beam and fastened a piece of wood to the bottom as a seat. I was blissfully happy swinging back and forth to the squeak, squeak noise of the ropes chafing against the beam when Granny appeared in the doorway. She looked as mad as a bull and swiftly slapped Aunt Jessie around the ear. "The girl is here in the shed playing 'titte me tortoise' instead of cleaning the house," she said to nobody in particular, while Aunt Jessie ran crying back into the house. I was too scared to ask what 'titte me tortoise' meant.

Saturday also meant bath time and however hard I tried, I could not escape this ordeal. Every single drop of water had to be carried home from the pump or from the ditch. The tin bath was brought in and put in front of the fireplace in the front room. The fireplace was a half-open grate in which the fire was fuelled from the top. Beside it, heated by the open firegrate was a small cast iron stove or oven, on top of which all cooking and boiling of water took place. Numerous cast iron saucepans filled with water had to be warmed one by one on the little stove and tipped into the bath until there were a few inches of hot water in the bottom.

No cheating was allowed. Every bit of me had to scrubbed from head to toe. Granny saw to that. She kept a very close eye on me, and I knew from past and painful experience that if she took to scrubbing me herself, she would make little allowance between a scrubbing board and my skin. After the ordeal, I put on my weekly change of clothes.

Adults, it seemed to me, never bothered to take a bath - - as long as they washed their feet. Feet must have been important, I thought. For the rest, they just seemed to wash the bits they could easily get at.

Chapter 3

On Sundays all work stopped. Recreation for the women was to sit under the huge chestnut tree facing the Green, showing off their clean Sunday aprons, and to have a good-ol' gossip, cackling like broody hens, all day long. Babies in baby carriages, or in a wooden box with wheels on, were liberally dotted around the shade of the tree. Amongst the village women somebody was always pregnant:

"Ya know what's amiss with her? She is'a breedin' young buns."

"I wonder who that belongs to?"

"Not -- --? I don't like he at all"

"I thought it was he."

"Did you see old so-and-so coming out of there the other day?"

Oh boy, they had a lovely time. There was always somebody's misdemeanour to be dissected. Invariably someone had morally fallen by the wayside.

After all it was Sunday. No ashes were cleared out, dishes were not washed up, everything was left till Monday. If we dared to work on Sundays, surely the corn would have caught fire. So nobody dared -- which suited us very well indeed.

On Sunday nights, everybody went to church and the rector would breathe fire and brimstone all over us.

The women donned their bonnets, or hats, and waddled off to church, their skirts sweeping the dirt paths as they moved along. The menfolk, wearing their best jackets, greased shoes, but often still in their rough and muddy 'working' corduroy trousers with leather straps buckled below the knee, would follow behind. The church was invariably filled to bursting point.

On this particular Sunday, one quite well-off parishioner, who liked to put on airs and graces, arrived late. That was undoubtedly to enhance her entrance by allowing every parishioner to have a fine view of her new feathered hat. She stood in the centre of the aisle, apparently looking for a seat, for a remarkably long time.

The Reverend Thomas looked over the rim of his spectacles, in the manner only parsons do, his face showing extreme disdain at the commotion created by the latecomer. Reluctantly everybody moved along on the bench, and the 'befeathered' lady popped her large behind into a space at the end of the pew, right in front of where Granny and Liz Holgate were sitting.

The colourful feathers of her impressive headgear swayed jauntily as she settled herself in -- and they touched one of the three candles which were lit at the end of each pew to ease the gloominess. All worshippers rose and started to sing the first hymn. Several of the men amongst whom I was standing, sang a tuneless version of 'some' hymn which bore little, if any, resemblance to the music or text of the hymn sheet they held upside down in their rough hands. I smiled a little, but there was no point in telling them to turn their sheets, for they could not read. Nor sing for that matter.

Granny nudged Liz Buckle. The feathers had caught fire and up went the hat. Sparks and smoke. Quickly, Liz Buckle snatched the hat, put it in the aisle and stamped on it until the fire was out. Suddenly, Granny stooped down, extracted one long feather which had not burned to cinders and stuck it back in its owner's hair. To be in church without headcover was not 'proper'.

During all this, the rector glared from the pulpit at his errant flock with a thunderous expression; hellfire would surely descend upon us all. Yet the congregation had carried on singing the hymn without interruption!

The parish of Matching provided a very poor living for its vicar. The tithes from Matching were endowed, or to use the ecclesiastical term, were impropriate to Felsted school and consequently the vicar was at the mercy of the school trustees for his sparse allowance.

The adjoining parish of Little Laver, on the other hand, had a rector rather than a vicar. Rector was the title given to the incumbent of a parish where the tithes were not impropriate, and in Little Laver the rector had a splendid living.

The rectory was a grand and prosperous place. It was a very large white house or mansion, set back from the road in its own extensive grounds. Quite how the few souls of Little Laver, with a dozen houses at best, could support such a grand set-up, was always a mystery to me in my early childhood when the Reverend Beauchamp was the rector of Little Laver.

In his devotion to his parishioners, this man of the cloth had paid rather too much homage to one particular member of his flock. In a most impious way, the girl, Alice Pavitt, promptly fell pregnant. I guess there are things which cause even a rector to forget his holy orders. Quite how he could is a mystery to me, for the Pavitt's house was like a cave -- cleanliness was not their first priority.

I remember Reverend Beauchamp well, but this particular incident took place before my birth: The Irreverent Beauchamp had provided the local women with Sunday gossip material for years: "What do you expect being married to that horrible old woman who never even looks female," I heard them say many years later.

The village was alive with lurid details. The story was furiously fired and kept alive by explicit newspaper reports when the bastardy proceedings went to court.

Reverend Beauchamp had apparently given Alice half-a-crown and threateningly remarked to her, "Don't you go and tell anyone what I have done to you." When it became apparent, however, that Alice was pregnant, Reverend Beauchamp tried to cover his rear. An extract from the court reports as printed in the local newspaper reads as follows:

Essex County Chronicle, Friday August 29th 1902
Rector of Little Laver Summoned
By a Single Women

He [Beauchamp] appeared to have gone to the house with a piece of paper, folded down and absolutely blank, and he got Alice Pavitt to sign her name upon it. He then asked her mother to put her name down also. As the other could not write, she made a cross and Alice wrote her name. They knew nothing of what was on the paper and believed that the rector would do something for them or the child. The paper was produced in court, containing the following declaration which the defendant, Reverend Beauchamp claimed was written at the cottage: I, Alice Pavitt, hereby declare the accusation made against the Rev. S.C. Beauchamp is untrue. and I withdraw any imputation of any improper conduct with him; and also declare that I have received no pecuniary or other compensation from him for signing this declaration. Dated this 5th day of May, 1902

Alice Pavitt

Witness: Eliza Pavitt

X her mark

Witness of the above: S.C. Beauchamp

The defendant denied that any impropriety had taken place between him and the girl and having tricked the girl into signing a withdrawal of the accusation. He claimed that Alice's mother had said that she did not want to go into court and had asked him for some money 'to square it'. "I replied that I would do nothing", Reverend Beauchamp told the court. "I wrote the withdrawal of the accusation on the paper in the house before I handed it to them to sign. The paper was not folded so that the writing was invisible."

He claimed that he was sure that he had not written the paper before he went into the cottage, but right there and then and with the same pen and ink as that with which the two women had signed.

The doctor who attended Alice in her confinement threw some doubt on the girl's paternity claim. He stated that the child when born had looked like a 'full term baby' and not a seven and a half month child which it would have been if the rector fatheredthe child.

The case was dismissed as there was not sufficient corroborative evidence. Alice's legal council asked for a re-hearing of the case as he had further witnesses to bring forward. The application was granted and the case came to court the following year -- Reverend Sidney Charles Beauchamp was committed for trial charged with perjury. Legal representation for the complainant, Alice Pavitt, was funded by the Earl of Desart, the public prosecutor for the county of Essex. The detailed press coverage continued:

Essex County Chronicle, Friday, January 16, 1903
The Little Laver Scandal
Rector Charged With Perjury

Two independent county analysts were called as witnesses by the prosecution and testified that the document has been written with two different kind of inks -- one was blue black, and one is common penny-a-pot ink.

News of the World, Sunday, January 18, 1903
Village Scandal
Essex Vicar Sent For Trial

Beuachamp's medical doctor appeared as witness for the defence. " I consider him highly nervous," he explained. "He suffered from influenza 13 years ago, had an attack of brain fever 23 years ago, was totally deaf in the right ear and the hearing in his left ear is very imperfect. Before the case came to court last year my patient was in a highly nervous state and suffered from almost complete sleeplessness". The witness added: "Mr Beauchamp, after the case, went on my advise to take the waters at Buxton." The defence lawyer enquired of the witness: Do you think an attack of brain fever more than 23 years ago would affect his ability to tell the truth in this court? The reply was: " It would affect his brain permanently, and I also believe that no one who has ever had influenza severely is the same person afterwards."In the witness's opinion the defendant had been quite unable to grasp the meaning of the questions asked.The defendant was committed to take his trial by jury at the next Essex Assizes.

Daily Mail, Sunday, January 18,1903
Rector Sent For Trial
Essex Clergyman's Explanation Of His Evidence

The defendant admitted that he had written the document in question at home and took it to the Pavitts cottage for signature. On the day of the trial he admitted making several mistakes in his evidence. He was deeply grieved that he should have made them, and at once wrote to his bishop on the matter.

The Times, Wednesday, February 11, 1903
"Rex v. The Rev. Sidney Beauchamp"

We are requested to state with reference to the report of his case in The Times of February 6, that in the course of the trial - which resulted in the jury finding the defendant *"Not guilty"* of the charge of perjury for which he was indicted - it was elicited in cross-examination by Mr Kemp, K.C., on behalf of the defendant, that the prosecutrix Alice Pavitt had been delivered of a child of which she alleged he was the father,on June 14, 1902 and that according to the medical evidence that the child was a "full term child", a fact which negatived the suggestion that the defendant could have been the father of the child as alleged by the girl.

The Reverend Beauchamp and his wife were thereafter totally ousted from local society. He continued to preach in his now rather empty church, but moved away several years later.

Somehow, I don't think the Reverend Beauchamp was too bright. I remember him pruning his apple trees, and cutting off the branch he was sitting on. 'Plomp', down on to the rectory lawn -- and the doctor had to be sent for.

On another occasion, he had shot a pheasant. As it dropped out of the sky like a stone, he stepped forward to catch it. Thump -- it hit his jet black 'cake tin' hat and the bridge of his nose. "He should have known better," the squire, who was watching grumbled, adding: "Not the form, you know."

Alice Pavitt was forced to bring up son, Freddie, on her own. And Freddie was never known to us as Freddie. Everybody just called him 'Beauchamp'.

At about the same time, Alice Pavitt's father was also taken to court. He was charged with stealing oats from his employer, a local farmer.

As was customary, the weekly allowance for oats to feed the horses on the farm had been issued to Pavitt. Pavitt had doled out too many oats to the horses early in of the week and by midweek had run out. The farm overseer had observed him going into the granary to get some more oats, reported it to the farmer and thus poor old Pavitt was charged with stealing oats.

This must surely have been one of the most unjust laws ever passed - feeding the farmer's horses in excess of the stipulated ration was considered stealing - even though Pavitt had had no personal gain. He was fined half a crown.

Some years later the Pavitts came to work for my employer, Henry Lucking and lived at Waterman's End cottage. They were, even to my eyes, a primitive lot: One day I found old Pavitt hobbling into the farm yard.

"What's the matter," I asked him. "Why are you hobbling?"

"Alice scraped my fit [feet] last night," came the pained reply. "Now my fit hurt even more."

Scraping of the feet meant literally what it says. Woollen socks, grime and skin had become so fused together that they had to be scraped off the feet. These simple old country people did not even know that just a modicum of personal hygiene would have avoided the need for feet scraping.

Chapter 4

Perry Cottage was set slightly back from the Green's edge. It was reached by walking down a broad path, which we referred to as the yard. The entrance to the neighbouring houses, the Holgates and the Whitbreads, on either side was also from the same yard.

It has always been known as Perry Cottage because for as long as anybody could remember it has always been occupied by a Perry. **The origin of the family name 'Perry', I have been led to believe, stems from 'The Dweller Near A Pear Tree'.**

This description is apt enough as there was indeed a lovely Williams pear tree right outside the back door of Perry Cottage. It has stood there all my life and fell down only last year. Given the family name, we shall replant one. It is good to know that my ancient ancestors also had the sense to live near a pear tree.

I have often wondered what the families were called who lived near an apple tree. Cox? Pippin? Orchard? Surely there were more apple trees in ancient Britain than Smiths!

The pear tree was Granny's pride and joy.

"Ya may have those that has fallen on the ground, nit t'others," she would say to me, pointing her finger warningly.

She would pick the pears most carefully and store them. Sometimes she was able to sell some as it was well known in the neighbourhood that our pears were lovely.

Granny had a quarter peck measure which she level filled with pears and then added a couple on the top. The quarter peck measure (1/2 gallon) was made of tree bark and held about a dozen medium-sized pears. Granny would put the pears in a paper bag and ask me to deliver them and return with the payment of four pence.

On a few occasions Granny was made very angry by suggestions from her pear purchasers that she had short weighed them.

"That bloody boy again!" she growled angrily.

"Ya'r little sod! Ya ate one of they, didn't ya?" she would scold.

And indeed it had been me. Those lovely, shiny yellow pears had been peeping at me out of the bag. Depending on the length of the walk, a few invariably proved irresistible.

Regrettably, I didn't get the chance too often though. Granny made sure of that.

"If they want them, they'll have to come here to get them," she said.

Grandfather had been born at Perry Cottage and had brought Granny there as a young bride. Granny had been born in the workhouse a mile and a half away down the High Laver Road and had met Grandfather after she had been sent into service at a local house.

Actually, to call it Perry Cottage was slightly misleading, as it was originally known as number one and number two Perry Cottages. Under the long, low thatched roof of Perry Cottage were what Granny called two 'housen'. Not until many years later, when I bought Perry Cottages, did it become one house.

My Granny and Grandfather lived in the left-hand cottage and the Holgates' grandparents lived in the right-hand cottage. The grandmother, Sally Holgate, was known as 'Long Sall', and we called her husband Grandpa Holgate.

Both cottages were identical in size and layout. You entered through the front door and stepped straight into the main room, known as the 'house', with a fireplace on the left wall and the door through to the kitchen, or the 'buttery' as we called it, on the right. Granny's and Grandfather's wheelbacked wooden chairs stood either side of the fireplace. The other pieces of furniture consisted of a dilapidated sofa and a table with an odd assortment of chairs.

If you walked from the front door straight through the 'house', you would find yourself facing the back door leading to the large garden. The garden was primarily filled with Grandfather's vegetable plots, but it also led to the privy.

The bedroom upstairs was reached via the staircase from the buttery. Under the staircase was the coal storage area, or 'cull'us' [coal house]in Granny's language.

Once a week Granny would walk the five miles to the nearest small town, Harlow, for her shopping. What we knew as Harlow, is now known as the village of Old Harlow. The present town Harlow was later build adjacent to it. Once a year Granny took me along and I would marvel at the 'metropolis' of Old Harlow.

"Anne Perry," Long Sall called over to Granny, "I'll come shopping with you today. My man is hard up for boots. I must get him a pair of boots."

Together they set off for the long walk and in due course arrived at their destination, the 'big shop' of Jacobs and Archibald. When the shop assistant attended to them, Granny was surprised to hear Long Sall ask to see some particular piece of cloth which she knew all too well that Long Sall could not afford. "What was Long Sall up to?" Granny asked herself.

The shop assistant clambered downstairs to fetch the requested items. As soon as his back was turned, Long Sall produced a knife and swiftly cut down one of the boots which were displayed hanging from the ceiling. She must surely have scouted out on a previous occasion where the right size was hanging, because Grandpa Holgate was a small and bent, thin-legged man, and would not have fitted the average man's boot. The boot had only just disappeared under her voluminous clothing, when the shop assistant returned.

"Never mind," Long Sall muttered to Granny, "I'll just have to send him again down the stairs again for something else." She expressed her dissatisfaction with the material and asked to be shown something else. As soon as the shop assistant's back was turned, Long Sall quickly cut down a second boot and it had likewise disappeared by the time he reappeared.

"No thank you, that's not right neither," Long Sall said, and left the shop dragging Granny along with her.

All the way home, Long Sall was laughing about the ease of her shopping expedition. "They are such fools, these shopkeepers," she exclaimed, "I can always get the better of them." Only when she got home did she discover that she had cut down two identical boots, both left-footed.

But she was quite right. Most of the time Long Sall did get the better of the shopkeepers. I have seen many a loaf of bread disappear under her apron while somebody else was talking to the baker.

Most people were known by their nicknames. Long Sall's real name was Sally and in this case the origin of the nickname was fairly obvious as she had a long solemn face. She looked as if all she could ever manage was to drag herself up the yard. She looked just like a childhood illustration of a witch. If you saw her today you would be terrified, particularly if you saw her carrying a broomstick.

The reason for a nickname was not always transparent. Nobody had any idea why Long Sall's husband, whom we children called Grandpa Holgate, was called 'Sofie' by the adults. Often the nickname went back to early childhood days and the origin was not even known to the bearer of the name. Yet the nickname stayed with them all through life. One of Sofie Holgate's brothers was called 'Buckle'. Buckle's wife was never known as Liz Holgate, but as Liz Buckle. One of Long Sall's children was known as 'Shippy' and one of her brothers as 'Hoddy'.

Long Sall's and Sofie's Holgates grandchildren, my childhood friends next door, answered to Fringie, Candles and Jim Smoke. Their mother, even though a big cheerful looking women herself, had produced rather frail children. Fringie, whose real name was Charlie, was named after a tiny wizened old engine driver, Fringie Bosworth, from the next village because as baby he was reputed to have looked just like him. Candles was so called because somebody had said of him that he had not been strong enough to blow a candle and Jim Smoke had been so fragile that a whiff of smoke could have blown him over.

One of the local farm labourers was called 'Flea Brooster' another one 'Bum And Scratch It'. There was 'Hoss [Horse] Whitbread' who worked with horses. His wife was known as Nell Hoss and their daughter was known as Bonker. Others of the Whitbread family were known as Beanie, Sammy Dinkham and Sergeant, even though Sergeant had never been in the army or police force. Gorby and Bodger lived next door to each other on Matching Green and the Blacksmith was called 'Ghonk' as he had a huge nose.

A local farmer laid down with his missus after drinking a whole bottle of whiskey one night. When their son was born nine months later, he was for forever after known as 'Whiskey'. At Waterman's End Cottage lived a father and son with the names of Nimmy and Nabby Pavitt. I never knew their real christian names .

To the best of my knowledge neither Granny nor my Grandfather had nicknames. They were John and Ann Perry. My grandfather was a thatcher and together with his colleague, George Peacock, he had walked far and wide practising his trade. There was always plenty of work for a thatcher. Houses and barns were still largely thatched, and after harvest, cornstacks and clamps had to be thatched to protect them from the winter. But when Grandfather got older and tired of the constant travelling, he took a job at Man Wood Farm and worked on the land.

At the end of each working day I waited longingly for Grandfather to come home. I would linger patiently by our gate, awaiting the appearance of his familiar figure round the corner of the Green by the post office. I could hear the men coming towards me from a long way off. Their heavy decker boots were fitted with steel caps and hobnails and made a distinctive click clack sound as they walked. Grandfather wore the traditional farm worker's attire of a braided, khaki-coloured smock, which almost reached to the knee and saved jackets from a lot of wear and tear. Their corduroy trousers had straps tied below the knee. The straps were largely used to save the trouser knees from excessive wear, but they also came in useful in preventing rats running up your trouser legs during threshing.

As soon as I spotted Grandfather I would run as fast as my three or four year old legs would carry me across the Green. Slung over his shoulder was the woven straw bag which, when he left for work well before six in the morning, contained his food and drink for the day: something for his morning break, bread and cheese for his lunch, and always a bottle of milkless tea.

Grandfather was an amiable and kind man and I loved him dearly. "There you go, little met'," he said, opening his straw bag and handing me the cheese rinds he had, as usual, saved from his lunch. He had also waited for his own treat until this moment. He lit up his clay pipe, I munched my cherished cheese rinds and companionably we trundled home together.

"Which horse did you take out today, Grandfather? Was it Bonny or was it Boxer? Why didn't you use Daisy? Which cart did you use?" the questions would impatiently pore out from me. My curiosity, particularly about the horses -- all of which I knew individually by name -- was insatiable. Grandfather would patiently tell me what each horse had done during that day, which implement had been used and what they had been fed. I was so fond of the horses that my Aunt Jessie had cut some paper in the shape of a horse for me. Sometimes when I was very lucky she'd find and cut out a horse picture from a newspaper or journal. If you squashed the legs of these paper horses very gently you could make them stand upright in a corner. My paper horses had exactly the same names as the horses Grandfather worked with.

On our walk home Grandfather would invariably be carrying a piece of wood over his shoulder, which he would have picked up in a copse or from a hedge. These pieces of wood which the men brought home were known as the 'shoulder bit'. As soon as we reached home Grandfather would inspect his garden and then saw up the shoulder bit and add it to our pile of firewood.

Thereafter we ate our tea while Granny gave us a rundown of the latest gossip she had heard, or Grandfather told what had happened on the farm that day. During the summer when the evenings still were light, Grandfather would after tea return to his vegetable garden and do a little more work, but in the winter when there was only one, or at best two, candles alight, by seven o'clock it was nearly time to go to bed.

I invariably knew when it was time to go to bed. Grandfather gave the signal by first taking his toe rags off and carefully laying them on the hob beside the fire. Toe rags were wrapped around the feet to save the socks from wear and tear. And then, as the last act of the day, he would wind the big clock hanging on the wall opposite the fireplace.

Granny often told us the story of how she had bought the clock with a clothes prop. Apparently she had walked the eight miles to Bishops Stortford to get something or other from a shop. While walking around the town, she came across a German firm selling clocks. They had been very persuasive, - in particular the proprietor whom Granny called Mr Heronback, - that she should have one of their magnificent clocks. These thirty-hour timepieces were manufactured by Jerome & Co of New Haven, Connecticut. For a mere threepence deposit, they said, it was going to be hers. Hence, Granny arrived home having bought the clock.

Hardly surprising, with thirteen children and her husband's income of eleven shillings, Granny never quite managed to get the money together for the subsequent instalments. Often, Long Sall gave warning that the collector man was going around the village and Granny would disappear into the privy in the garden, or the spider villa as she called it. Finally she got fed up with being asked for money she couldn't possibly afford and told Long Sall:

"Ya just wait and see. I hen't got any money. I'll drive that old bugger away."

As she saw the money collector walk down our yard, she grabbed the clothes prop which had just moments before been holding up the washing line and walked threateningly towards him: "Ya come one step further and I'll drop this prop over yar head. Ya ma'k ma words."

The money collector was obviously not going to take any chances, confronted by two such fierce old women -- angry Granny, supported by Long Sall, who looked quite like an old witch without even trying. He was never seen again. "Sa'rved him right," were always Granny's last words about the clock.

We still have the big clock today and whenever I look at it I am reminded of Granny's clothes prop and Grandfather's evening ritual of winding the clock. It works fine, but I ought to have it seen to. It is just as likely to strike twenty as two.

Grandfather's only indulgence seemed to be his pipe. When he was not at work, he was out working in the garden. Every square inch of the garden was planted with vegetables. Because Grandfather was not a drinking man, I remember so well the one occasion when he got drunk. The local gentry had organised a party on the Green to celebrate the coronation of George V in 1910. Free food and drink were plentiful and the villagers had a very cheerful and carefree time. Grandfather had drunk a few glasses of beer, but because he was so unused to alcohol he fell over and hit his head on the coal shed. Granny reckoned that his health was never quite right again after that fall.

In Granny and Grandfathers days' doctors were not easily available to the poor. Most poor people died without the attention of a doctor. If you heard that somebody amongst the villagers had called in the doctor you knew that there was very little hope for them. They plainly could not afford to have medical help and invariably left it far too late.

While most doctors were immensely compassionate, they could not visit a patient unless told that a villager was ill. Some doctors were also reluctant to deal with patients under these primitive and unhygienic conditions. The poor hardly lived in better conditions than animals. The doctors also knew that, just as likely as not, they would never be paid for their services.

Sometimes, in dire emergencies, a parish doctor was assigned to visit the sick person. The bill would have to be sent to the local board of guardians of the Rural District Council for approval and if authorised, would be paid out of parish funds.

Villagers who were a little better off would join the 'Slate Club'. This was one way people tried to help themselves. A meeting would be held and it was decided what each person had to pay into the Slate Club each week. A trusted member of the community, who could read and write, was put in charge and he would chalk up the names of the members and their subscriptions on a big slate board in the pub. From the funds collected in this way, the Slate Club would help members in distressed situations when a doctor or an undertaker was needed to be paid. The remainder of the monies were shared out before Christmas which helped to provide a few extra treats for the festive season.

Grandfather had so very much been looking forward to benefiting from Asquith's Old Age Pension plan which had been introduced in 1908. Not that any of the old people had understood it at first. They were baffled and, to some extent, even suspicious. Why should anybody want to give them money just because they were old? They were used to working until they dropped. If they could not work any longer, for reasons of ill health, for example, and their children were unable to help as they could barely feed their own hungry brood, they had to go into the poor-house.

Retirement was a word which did not exist in their vocabulary. But eventually when the over-seventy year olds did go to the post office to draw their pensions, they were elated.

One of my uncles who went to get his pension -- and had his belief that the talk of old age pension was just propaganda pleasantly shattered -- came out of the post office with five shillings and bought me a whole paper cone filled to the brim with sweets. A whole penny's worth of Black Jacks -- I have remembered Asquith with fondness ever since.

Grandfather, however, did not survive long enough to see his pension dream come true.

Grandfather died when I was eight years old. A pony trap hearse arrived to take him away. Granny and her children, my uncles and aunts, climbed into the brougham which followed behind. The other mourners fell in behind the cortege and walked the one and a half miles to High Laver Church.

I was considered too young to go along to the funeral. But I knew, if they meant what they said, that Grandfather had gone away for ever, I was going to miss him terribly.

After Grandfather's death, Granny had to manage on even less money. There was simply not enough to feed and clothe us. In sheer desperation Granny applied for 'parish relief'. To her absolute delight it was granted: the relieving officer arrived and brought her two shillings -- the sum she was to receive every week from now on.

Her burden would be a little easier. Granny was overjoyed and wanted to celebrate this marvellous event: her eyes were bright and she was smiling broadly as she called: "Boy, go to the Chequers and get me half a pint of porters." Clutching the four pence tightly in my hand, I rushed to the Chequers to get Granny her rare treat -- a glass of frothing stout. Carefully balancing the glass in order not to spill a single drop, I carried it back.

Alas, her joy was shortlived. Granny cursed furiously: "That old sod next door. I wish she would mind her own business." A neighbour had reported Granny for spending her parish relief money on the 'demon alcohol' and the allowance was promptly stopped. Thank God, the parson intervened. He was a sensible sort of man, and after he had pointed out just how poor we were, the relief was restored.

Chapter 5

Matching Fair took place each year, on the 1st October. Gaily and garishly painted horse-drawn caravans would arrive and spill their contents of fairground folks, children, animals and equipment on to our village green.

Matching Fair was anticipated with a great deal of delight and excitement, and also with some trepidation by the adults, who did not altogether trust these travelling people. But on the whole, the fair was welcomed as a great annual event with much merry-making.

A few days before the start of the fair, all livestock and horses were cleared off the Green and the task of setting up the amazing stalls and fun activities began.

My friends and I watched this transformation of our Green with immense fascination. All around the Green a wondrous array of stalls appeared in no time at all. Great big steam engines trundled across the grass, leaving deep tracks, and took their position to power the various fun rides. The only area which was kept clear was the cricket ground and pavilion.

First, the big round base of the carousel was put into position. One by one, the brightly coloured and gilded horses on their long wooden poles were secured in their places. The striped canopy was put on, the sign 'Greenaway -- Steam Galloping Horses' was fixed to the top, and finally -- we could hardly wait -- the multicoloured lights were switched on. The organ struck up a merry tune and the carousel was transformed into a magic place of glamorous rides.

The village green now sparkled brilliantly and cheerful tunes played invitingly. People, dressed in their best togs, walked for miles to Matching Green from the outlying farms and surrounding villages. Everybody had looked forward to the fair for weeks. This was the great event at the end of summer.

I had worked back-breakingly hard after school at picking potatoes for one penny a day and with eight pence in my pocket, I was ready to enter the kaleidoscopic world of the fair. So many things on offer! What should I spend my money on first? The candy floss stall? The roundabout? The hoopla stall? Possibly my arms were still too short to throw the rings around wonderful objects laid out on the table? No, better save my money for something else. Everything seemed gleaming and glamorous. Squires, farmers and workers alike paraded around, having a very jolly time of it.

I watched several grown-up men try their luck at the 'Trial of Strength' stall. They lifted the big mallet high into the air and hit on the peg, whilst grunting loudly from the exertion. Sometimes, the ball shot up high enough to set off the bell at the top of the pole with a 'ping'. These successful strong men were greatly admired and strutted around while the girls giggled and called encouragement to the next one to pick up the mallet.

No, that wasn't for me either. First, pick up some candy floss, then have another perusal.

The pink balls bouncing on top of the water fountain at the rifle range caught my eye.

"No, little met'," Uncle George said, suddenly appearing beside me, "You better wait until I have taught you how to shoot. Then you can take any one of these things home with you."

I looked up at Uncle George longingly: "When will you teach me to shoot?" I admired my Uncle George greatly. He was one of the best shots I have ever known.

"When you are a little bit older, little met'. I'll teach you then," he said, ruffled my hair and walked on.

Jack Holgate joined me and together we ran off to have a go at the swings -- and then to take a ride on the carousel --

and then to throw a ball at the puppets -- and then to buy some fudge -- and then, suddenly, my eight pence were gone, with three more days of the fair to go.

I ran home with tears streaming down my face. The exciting world of the fair was waiting for me and I had no money left. Mother, who was on leave from service at the time, slapped my hand for having spent my money so recklessly. She disapproved of the fair. Too much riffraff about for her liking. But then she softened and gave me a florin [two shillings - ten pence in today's decimalised currency and then a small fortune for a child] so I could have another go.

The fair also served as a trading place for all sorts of things, including labour. Men walked around indicating their occupation in various ways: a shepherd would have a bit of wool sticking from his button hole, and a horsekeeper would be wearing a horse ribbon. The carter often carried the mark of his trade, a whip, and the stockman would be wearing his working clothes of beetle tail jacket and bowler hat. To be stockman was a very exalted position in the hierarchy of farm labour. They were able to wear their beetle tail jackets as they were indoors most of the time. If it rained, snowed or hailed, they could watch it from inside the cowshed standing cosily knee deep in straw. Farm labourers, meanwhile, would be outside in any weather protected only by an old corn sack tied around their shoulders or over their heads.

During the fair, farmers looking for a new man could have an informal chat with any potential job searcher, leave it at that or strike a deal with him.

Many men met their future wives for the first time at Matching Fair. It was a wonderful occasion to meet other young people from the district. The fair provided a rare opportunity. After all, courting was mostly done on foot and distance put a limit to how many girls you could encounter. That's why the same names kept appearing right through the neighbourhood. There were many Perrys, Holgates and Whitbreads.

As we boys grew a little older, the fair and its gaiety took on a quite different significance. There were some lovely girls amongst the fairground people; often dark-haired and gypsy-looking, and with a gay abandon which the village girls would not have dared to display for fear of being clouted around the ear by their mothers or aunts. The fairground girls, however, were well versed in the facts of life. Whatever we hadn't known before, we learned during Matching fair.

By midnight on the 4th October, the laws stipulated that the fair be moved. Newly won ornaments were proudly placed on mantelpieces and normality returned to the village.

But sometimes, if the fair had not moved too far away, some of the older boys who were fortunate enough to own bicycles, would in their free time follow the fair, or rather the sloe-eyed girls, around for a week or two.

It has always puzzled me how all of Granny's thirteen children could look, and be, quite so different. Some looked as if they had been born under a hedge, while others were quite aristocratic. Occasionally a sneaking suspicion entered my mind, that Granny may have paid off the odd debt in this way. Some of her children looked nothing like Grandfather. But I am quite sure that if Granny would have heard me make any such suggestion, my behind would have become black and blue.

Uncle Jimmy was Granny's youngest son and he was a very good looking chap. Tall, handsome -- and I adored him. However tired he might have been after work, he always found time and energy to play with me. There was never very much time for us children to play. There were always a multitude of tasks to be done and things we had to help with. And, of course, straight after school there was always water to be fetched from the pump. Apart from that, Granny did not approve very much of playing. Play was a total waste of time in her mind.

"Ma'k ma words," she would say. "Nothing good will come of that."

Granny had been born in the local workhouse and, I am quite sure, had never in her childhood been able to indulge in play. From a very early age she had only known work, work and more work. Workhouse children had to earn their keep as poverty was considered a crime, which deserved a stigma, and the poor were poor not because providence had ordained them to be so but purely as a result of their own failings. Workhouses after all had been mixed receptacles of misery, where every class of pauper, vicious or unfortunate, young or old, sick, well or lunatic, was dumped. Granny had been luckless enough to be born there as her unmarried mother had nowhere else to turn when she had fallen pregnant. Her father, a prosperous widowed farmer who lived within sight of the workhouse at High Laver Hall Farm, obviously had no intention of supporting mother and child. Only in workhouses could an able-bodied person get relief, and in order to deter them, as funds needed for these institutions were bitterly resented by the parish, the regime was purposely made repugnant.

It was not until 1891, nearly thirty years after my Granny had left the workhouse, that the poor law governing workhouses was amended to permit the provision of toys and books for these institutions.

Granny had undoubtedly been shown very little affection in this harsh environment and even with me, her little grandson, whom she brought up and whom she unquestionably loved, it was clearly not easy for her to show physical affection. A pat or a ruffle of the hair was all she could manage

My Uncle Jimmy was quite different. He would hug and cuddle me. He always found the time to play with me as soon as he got home from work. Playtime was from the moment he had returned until Granny called us in for supper. My very favourite game was to play farming. Farming was all around me. Almost everybody I knew worked on the land or in some or other capacity on a farm.

Sometimes on dark, wet evenings Uncle Jimmy would take me into the shed attached to our cottage. There he would set to work sharpening his tools. Or sometimes he would make a wonderful toy for me. He would light the candle in a small lantern and hang it overhead and place another candle in a jam jar on the workbench. I thought this was very cosy. Just Uncle Jimmy and me! It was a real treat for me simply to be with him and watch him work. Just to be near him made me feel a very happy boy.

I especially recall the occasion when Uncle Jimmy brought home a wooden margarine box. He had called at the post office shop and bought it. These boxes were about eighteen inches by twelve inches in size and roughly six inches tall. They were readily available and most shopkeepers were only too pleased to have them taken off their hands for a penny. Uncle Jimmy mollified my anxious enquiries about the box by telling me that he intended to make a small replica of a farm wagon for me. He showed me the rough drawing where he had copied down the proportions of the wagon at the farm. And he promised, to my delight, that I could help him. What bliss! I looked tremendously forward to being with him while he made it. That would be just as nice as owning the wagon. As I now know, it is not always easy to get a job done with a little fellow trying to 'help'. Uncle Jimmy never scolded me and was always patiently ready to explain anything to me.

"Don't do that little met," he would say. "You might hurt yourself. Look, let me show you. Do it this way. If the tool should slip it won't catch your hands."

Uncle Jimmy had also bought four tins of Lyon's Golden Syrup - - two small ones and two large ones. Despite the fact that I was delighted to see this large supply of treacle, I was rather puzzled by the fact that he told me that we needed them to build the wagon. But he soon explained it to me.

"You see met," he said pointing at the drawing of the proposed wagon. "The front wheels on a wagon are smaller than the rear wheels. We are going the use the lids of the small treacle tins for the front wheels and the bigger ones for the rear."

Over many evenings Uncle Jimmy sawed and carved the wooden box into the shape of a wagon. He made a v-shaped draw-bar for it and attached it to the underside of the wagon with a wooden block which a large nail driven through it. This emulated a pivot, and the wagon could be steered. The axles, which the blacksmith had made for him from a bit of scrap iron, and wheels were fitted. All that remained to be done now was to paint the wagon like a proper farm wagon. Uncle Jimmy painted my beautiful little wagon in dark green with red wavy stripes down the side - - just like the real thing. I was very proud indeed and we played with it many an evening. After each play session my wagon was carefully put back into the shed.

The following summer he showed me how cornstacks are made.

"Come on met, we'll harvest our crop," he said taking my hand and led me into the garden. "As we don't have corn," he explained, "We shall make do with hay."

"Don't touch these tools," Uncle Jimmy pointed at the bagging hook, which had a very sharp 12" blade used to cut the grass.

"You are too young for that yet. But you can help me lay the bundles of grass out."

Uncle Jimmy moved along each path and cut the grass while I laid it in nice little swathes behind him making sure that the big ends of the grass all laid in the same direction. I loved the summery smell of the freshly cut grass. Then we would leave the swathes of grass to dry for a few days, checking them each evening. If the weather was nice and dry, the grass would be ready for turning after a few days. Once it was thoroughly dry, Uncle Jimmy built a proper stack for me - - a perfectly formed miniature version of the huge stacks which dotted the countryside after harvest. He worked skilfully, explaining his work to me all the time until the stack was about seven feet long and three feet wide - - and it was at least three feet tall as I had to stand on my tip-toes to see over it.

Looking back many years later, I rather think that Uncle Jimmy had still been a boy at heart. He seemed to take immense pleasure in making these things and sharing them with his small nephew.

"Come on little met," he would say as soon as he came home. "Let's see if our stack has settled. If not we may have to add some grass cuttings. It has to settle properly before we can thatch it."

Each evening Uncle Jimmy brought home a little straw and when he was satisfied with the stack, he thatched it, again all the while teaching me how it was done. I thought that my stack was the most beautiful building in Matching Green. I was tremendously proud of it. Surely no other eight year old had his very own thatched stack in the garden. Whenever Granny allowed it, I would bring some of my friends in the garden and show my wonderful stack off.

During the winter when the animals were short of natural food, Uncle Jimmy warned me that the time had come to reap the profit from our 'farming' enterprise. Even though I had been told all along that the stack would only be there for a while, it was long before I was ready for its demolition. I wanted to keep it for ever -- or at least until next summer when we could build a new one.

"No met. This is how farming works," Uncle Jimmy told me. "This is when the animals need the hay. Look over the fence, there is Bonny, the cart horse (belonging to a neighbour who ran a hay carting business). She is hungry. She will be pleased for this sweet hay. We'll sell it now."

To ease my pain at loosing the stack, Uncle Jimmy organised a day of 'mock' threshing. He turned our little coal cart, which he had some years earlier made from a wooden sugar box and pram wheels, upside down. A few planks were removed from the bottom and a sort of propeller fitted into the gap. He plaited some binder string and fashioned it into a drive belt. To stop me crying, Uncle Jimmy asked me to turn the handle which, somehow, with the help of his engineering, turned the propeller. Solemnly he proceeded to push the bundles of straw through the propeller and it fell in a heap at the bottom. From there he would scoop it up again and put it in bags ready to give it to the horsekeeper a couple of doors away. Today I am immensely grateful to think what trouble he took to entertain me, teach me and 'waste' a whole Sunday on pretend threshing the hay in order to stop me feeling too sad.

At other times many enjoyable hours were spent with Uncle Jimmy helping me with my school work and my boyish passion for drawing. He was a very good drawer and a had a whole collection of the drawing he made for me which I carefully stored in a box. Sometimes the schoolmaster would allow us to take a book or print home so we might copy it. I had brought a bird picture home and both Uncle Jimmy and I sat that evening and drew it. He drew a splendid bird, hardly surprisingly, much better than my own childish drawing. It looked every bit as nice as the original we had copied it from. Hence, next morning I took Uncle Jimmy's drawing to school with me instead of my own humble efforts.

"Children look at this wonderful drawing young Perry has made," the schoolmaster exclaimed. "Well done Perry. We'll have to hang that in a very special place."

This is the only time I have ever known Uncle Jimmy to be very cross with me. I told him what I had done. I had failed to tell the schoolmaster that I had not drawn the picture, but had been very pleased to be singled out for praise.

"That was wrong little met," he scolded me. "That was cheating. It's not right to cheat. Please don't ever do that again."

I didn't actually know what 'cheating' meant, but I had grasped that if Uncle Jimmy did not like it, it had to be wrong.

Many years later when the same schoolmaster taught my own children I was often tempted, -- but never did, -- to ask him why he had not given me away and reprimanded me. I am sure he must have known an adult drawing when he saw it. Possibly he felt that there was enough hardship and misery around without taking a little chap down a peg or two. Bless him - - I would have been mortified if he had.

I loved my Uncle Jimmy dearly and I was also immensely proud of my him. Not only was he a very good and clever at everything he touched, he was also the only man in Matching Green to own a gramophone.

It had been ordered from J. G. Graves of Sheffield and he was paying it off with a half a crown postal order per month. When the gramophone had arrived, Mr Wortley, the butcher, assembled it and we stared in wonderment at this wonderful magic box. Then, Uncle Jimmy placed the first record on the turntable, wound it up and carefully set the needle down. To our absolute delight, the most marvellous sounds came out of the huge horn. Granny clapped her hands and jumped up and down with excitement. She looked at the gramophone in amused bewilderment, and I clambered on my adored Uncle Jimmy's lap.

Many of the villagers had come half way down our yard attracted by the unaccustomed sound of music. There they stood and listened with us to the five records supplied with the gramophone.

We got an enormous amount of pleasure from listening to the gramophone. Sometimes Uncle Jimmy sent away for two new records at a cost of two shillings each. This was an awful lot of money, considering a man's wages were eleven shillings per week. He was able to afford such luxuries as records and always be well dressed because he was most careful with his money. He earned overtime pay and instead of spending it in the pub, he saved.

Some weeks after ordering, the new records would arrive by post in a box filled with sawdust and eventually we had a nice little music collection at Perry Cottage, which entertained us for countless hours. Granny particularly loved listening to the hymns, which Uncle Jimmy occasionally ordered especially to please her -- or to Billy Williams, the comedian singing:

> *When father papered the parlour,*
> *you couldn't see Pa for paste,*
> *dabbing it here, dabbing it there*
> *paste and paper everywhere.*
> *Mother was stuck to the ceiling,*
> *kids were stuck to the floor*
> *I have never seen such a blooming family so stuck up before.*

A few years later the First World War started and I remember the music on the records changing. Stanley Kirby had a song which went something like this:

We have watched you playing cricket and every kind of game,
at football, golf and tennis you men have made your name.
But now your country calls you to play your part in the war.
No matter what befalls you, we will love you all the more.
So come and join the forces, as your fathers did before.
We don't want to lose you, but we think you ought to go.
For your King and your Country, both need you so.
We shall love you, but miss you, but with all our might and mane,
We shall cheer you, may God bless you when you come back again.

Which of course many of them did not.

I am not sure if the grown-ups were aware of it, but I was certainly too small to notice that Uncle Jimmy was spending his hard-earned two shillings on war propaganda. But we played the records often enough for me to remember most of the words over eighty years later.

Uncle Jimmy's employer was Henry Lucking from Waterman's End, who also became my governor a few years later. As a farm worker, Uncle Jimmy was exempted from being called up for service during the First World War. But Uncle Jimmy wanted to go. Mr Lucking tried very hard to dissuade him from joining up but I guess the posters of Lord Kitchener, his finger outstretched -- Your King and Country Need You -- and seeing so many of his friends in uniform convinced Uncle Jimmy that it was his duty.

He was twenty two years old when he joined the Essex Regiment and took the King's shilling. It was at this time that Granny started to buy a daily paper. It was my first experience of newspapers, and I would sit with Granny and read out the casualty lists for her. Moreover, during the war years, Granny taught herself to read. She would ask me: "What's that?" She would never ask again: she had absorbed my explanation. Slowly but surely, she worked out how to read.

Uncle Jimmy was wounded in the leg during battle in France and was sent home to recuperate. When the papers arrived ordering him to rejoin his regiment my heart nearly broke. On the day Uncle Jimmy was to leave, I hid in the shed. I concealed myself behind some sacks of potatoes and cried and cried. I did not want Uncle Jimmy to leave. I was desperately scared of losing him.

By now, I knew what it meant, going to war, because virtually everyday, children at my school were crying. Somebody had lost a brother,

Uncle Jimmy - Alfred James Perry

64

a father or an uncle. I did not want to lose my beloved Uncle Jimmy. The shed door opened. I saw Uncle Jimmy standing against the light, his tall figure as upright as a dart and the badge on his cap gleaming in the darkness of the shed:

"Come on, metey, you have got to say goodbye," he said, and scooped me up for a big hug.

"Look after Granny, met, until I come home again," he said and walked off.

Not many weeks after Uncle Jimmy had rejoined his regiment, a telegram arrived:

WE REGRET TO INFORM YOU THAT PRIVATE
ALFRED JAMES PERRY NO 26768 OF THE
ESSEX REGIMENT IS DANGEROUSLY WOUNDED
WITH GAS SHELL WOUNDS IN NUMBER FOUR
GENERAL HOSPITAL STOP
REGRET PERMISSION TO VISIT CAN NOT BE
GRANTED STOP

While we were helping Granny to decipher this, our old postman came down the yard again bringing us another telegram:

REGRET PRIVATE ALFRED JAMES PERRY
NO 26768 OF THE ESSEX REGIMENT DIED OF HIS
WOUNDS IN NUMBER FOUR GENERAL
HOSPITAL STOP
STILL YOUR BOY AND STILL LOVING YOU STOP
SIGNED ABRIDGE REGIMENTAL PADRE
STOP

My beloved Uncle Jimmy, Alfred James Perry, Private 26768, 1st Battalion of the Essex Regiment died on Wednesday, 27th February 1918, aged 25.

This scroll and his service medal arrived some time later. It did not help in any way to soften my loss.

After Uncle Jimmy's death, Henry Lucking was very kind to Granny. He had been very fond of her son and, after all, Jimmy had been the main breadwinner in our family. Life was going to be very hard for Granny. Mr Lucking helped by giving her eggs and firewood. Once, he even gave her a 'sitting of eggs'. It is the only time I have ever known a hen to bring off a whole brood of chickens -- and each and every one of them a pullet. To my great sadness, Granny had to peddle them. I had been so fond of the hen and the little chicks. But Granny had a debt to settle and the chicks were sold for two shillings each. The higler man, a poultry man to whom Granny sold the chicks, came to our village regularly. He had an uncanny knack for knowing when somebody was hard up and he could grab a shilling.

We children lived with the war every day. Several anti-aircraft guns were positioned in our neighbourhood. We enjoyed collecting shrapnel. We were supposed to go indoors, of course, as soon as the guns sounded, but we managed to get closer to the gun positions than any of the adults or the gunners ever suspected. Our prize find was a nosecap. That would be nicely polished and placed on the mantelpiece.

Our sleep was constantly disrupted by the shrill whistles announcing an air raid alert, followed invariable by the sound of the anti-aircraft guns.

The Zeppelin, however, we knew was on its way long before we could see it. Its terrifying, menacing drone disrupted the quiet night. The searchlights from the anti-aircraft positions flitted across the night sky and everybody in the village rushed out on to the Green to see the spectacle.

Initially we experienced the thrill of the searchlights picking up the shape of a huge cigar in the sky. The Royal Flying Corps biplanes could be heard buzzing, heading off for their aerial combats and their attempts to pump bullets into the hull of the monster airship.

The difficulties for these early open biplanes were huge. They were largely constructed of wood, covered with fabric, held together with wire brazing. Flying at the best of times carried huge perils: Thick leather clothing and helmet, goggles and warm boots was all that protected the pilots in their open cockpits, engines were temperamental, -- there were few instruments and guns were prone to jamming.

Night flying was particularly unpredictable. No radio, no navigational or ground directional aids, or parachutes were available to these brave pilots. It would take some considerable time for them to reach the 13-14000 feet cruising altitude of the airship, by which time the Zeppelin might well have disappeared into thick cloud cover.

We considered the Huns to be absolute monsters who brought terror and grief. At any time a dozen or more airships might be flying over the Channel in the of direction England to drop their cargo of deadly bombs on our towns.

But on this fateful occasion, our pilots were successful and the Zeppelin took a direct hit. At first with incredulity, then with horror, we watched as the enormous monstrosity became engulfed in flames. Within seconds the entire airship was a blazing inferno. I don't believe that there was a single woman in Matching Green not crying as we watched the poor devils burn to cinders.

Bits of the main structure started to break away and fall to ground like flaming comets until only a fiery red skeleton was left. For about an hour we stood transfixed observing this human tragedy -- it was horrible.

At Matching Green we saw three Zeppelins burning through the war. One went down at Cuffley the second one at Billericay and the third one at Potters Bar.

TWO ZEPPELINS MEET THEIR DOOM.

BURNT AND WRECKED IN ESSEX.

A WONDERFUL MIDNIGHT SPECTACLE

In the early hours of Sunday morning two Zeppelins were brought down in Essex—one falling in flames in a field, and the other coming to earth, the crew being taken prisoners. The spectacle of the burning airship as it slowly fell in a burning mass which illuminated the whole sky was witnessed by countless thousands, and everywhere a mighty cheer went up as the monster met its doom.

Twelve German Zeppelins participated in the raid, which began on Saturday night, the airships attacking Lincolnshire and other Eastern Counties, and the outskirts of London. The latter attack, about midnight, was beaten off by aeroplanes and anti-aircraft guns. Bombs were dropped, however, and it is regretted that as a result of the raid 38 persons were killed and 125 injured.

THE ESSEX WEEKLY NEWS.
FRIDAY. SEPTEMBER 29. 1916.

A second Zeppelin came down and the crew a was luckier than the poor devils that had been burnt to death:

ESSEX VICAR & THE HUNS.

THE ESSEX WEEKLY NEWS. FRIDAY. SEPTEMBER 29. 1916.

The following additional particulars rela e to the capture:—

The crew of the Zeppelin. headed by their commander, named Boecker, were met by the Vicar of an adjoining parish. who volunteered to put them up in his Church Hall. Ho cycled ahead to inform his parishioners, but they resented the presence of the Huns. However, the Vicar told them that if they wished to make a demonstration they could run up the Union Jack, and give three cheers for the King. This was accordingly done. The Vicar's wife, who is the commandant of the V.A.D., had nurses and two cooks ready for the party.

Two of the men complained of burns on the head. three had damaged hands. one was cut on the fingers, and one had a broken rib. The commander grumbled about being herded with his men, and suggested that he should have private accommodation. A bedroom was made up at the Vicarage for the man with the broken rib. and a bed was provided for the commander behind a screen in the Mission Room, but the latter accommodation was not accepted. In the morning the injured man was taken to a military hospital. and the remainder of the crew to a detention barracks.

It is stated that a map of the district was found in a boot of one of the men, who. it is also stated. was formerly resident in the locality. The Germans were all well clothed, and several had very fine fur coats, capital, strong boots. and leather overalls. Most of them wore ordinary sailor caps, but some had peak and others knitted caps. The commander, of the typical Prussian type remained sulky during his stay, but his crew were very civil—almost obsequious, as Germans usually are when in the position of "under-dog." The second officer in command of the Zeppelin was given a copy of a London daily paper in order that he might see how the Germans are being beaten all along the line.

On the day the war ended, the church bells rang and men, ringing hand bells walked around the Green.

"Granny," I said, "they are telling us that the war is over."

She looked at me sadly, pulled me close to her side and gently patted me on the head:

"We have nothing to look forward to, metey. Have we?"

O dear, that was a terrible war. No, I shouldn't say that -- all wars are terrible. I am so pleased that neither my children nor my grandchildren have needed to experience war at first hand. The First World War lasted only four years, but it produced casualties on a scale which are scarcely comprehensible -- more than one million men lost their lives.

It is somewhat ironical that this appalling war with such an enormous loss of life should have led to an improvement of conditions at home. Those were the years when the first steps gingerly were taken towards a modern welfare state. By the end of the war the government was committed to form a Ministry of Health to coordinate health services and national insurance. Social reformers like William Beveridge were entering the scene. Especially after Lloyd George succeeded Asquith as Prime Minister in 1916, reform got on the move.

With hindsight, I can say that women in particular seem to have been major beneficiaries of that war. They made some headway. The suffragettes, who had gallantly fought for women's rights, finally got their way. Married women over thirty years of age were granted the vote in 1918. But even more importantly, thousands of women had served with distinction at the front as nursing officers, in war administration, ammunitions factories and many other jobs which had previously been only male occupations. These women would never fit back into their

71

previous, very subordinate roles. But as I say, that is looking at the period with the benefit of hindsight. At the time, when I started work in 1917, my concerns were quite different.

Thanks to Lloyd George and his conviction that child labour was being exploited, my pay almost doubled to six shillings and sixpence a week.

It seems to me, that Lloyd George cared more about us at the beginning of the century, than these silly blighters, who call themselves our parliamentary representatives, do now. This government is making such a hash of things. Possibly they have been in power for too long -- nearly fifteen years, and they treat us as if 'they' know what's best for us, the proletariat.

I can't vote for them again. And yet I can't possibly vote Labour, because they would ban all field sports, with fox hunting at the top of their list.

I have seen many fox hunts in my ninety years. But you know, in all this time, I have only ever known two foxes to be killed. Several times have I seen the fox stop, look over his shoulder, sit down, scratch his ear like a dog and lope off again. The hounds were in full cry but were nowhere near the fox and he didn't look particularly bothered.

Do these witless goons not realise what the English countryside would look like without field sports -- no hedges, copses or coverts. Meanwhile, it provides good exercise and employment for many thousands. These sports are part of country living. But as the tabloid press keeps informing us, politicians seem to be more interested in 'indoor' sports.

Then there is the urban brigade which feels they have the right to trample across the countryside with scant regard for private property. As if it is a inherent right for an Englishman to walk the countryside. They are most probably the same people who complain of the excessive noise pollution of their next door neighbour's cockerel's crow.

Yes, of course, the old bridlepaths should be maintained and kept accessible to all. Farmers have taken some advantage in this respect. In fact, I myself have recently 'reopened' a footpath. I walked along the trail which I used frequently as a child and which had been incorporated into a field.

But if these do-gooders have their way we will not have the trees and hedges and their wildlife habitat. We will all be taking our country walks peacefully together across prairie landscapes and bemoan the good old days.

And, for my taste, I'd much rather have wild pheasant for my supper than a battery hen or any other intensively farmed animal.

Almost immediately after my pay rise, Granny told me that I would now be allowed to keep sixpence as weekly pocket money -- my very own money.

Twelve years old and with a shining sixpence in my pocket, I decided that as a working man, I should call in at the pub. My friend George Blackmore and I walked down to the Cherry Tree pub.

George, being a little older, went inside and ordered two glasses of shandy for us. Feeling very much like one of the men, we sat in the garden of the pub and savoured our first drink.

News, however, travelled fast in Matching Green: "Yar boy's in the pub." Somebody told granny and when I reached home some time later, she was standing in the doorway, battle-axe expression on her face and hands on her hips: "Ya've been to drink." And with that she raised her arm and with all her might clouted me round the ear. The force deprived my of breath and threw me backwards crashing into the back door. If the door had not been closed, I would surely have landed at the bottom of the garden.

I never quite got over this onslaught and I have been a very infrequent visitor to pubs ever since. Somehow, I never lost sight of Granny's lesson that spending one's hard-earned money on drink is a total waste.

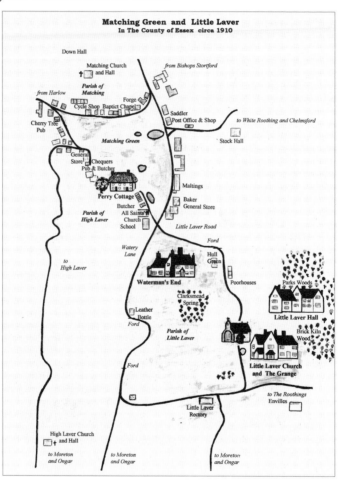

Matching Green and Little Laver
In The County of Essex circa 1910

Chapter 6

Squire -- a wealthy gentleman called Herman James Meyer owned the estate on which my entire working life was spent -- the farms and land known as Waterman's End, Little Laver Grange and Little Laver Hall.

Squire's tenant farmer Henry Lucking, who had picked me off the school bench in 1917 aged twelve, was thus my employer -- even though in the early years I was never quite sure who my master was.

Sometimes, particularly in the shooting season, I would be working for Squire and during the busy farming season for Henry Lucking.

It was even more difficult to attempt a guess as to who would be paying me my wages on Friday evenings.

I must assume that they had some sort of system, because from whichever source, my wages never failed to materialise.

Waterman's End is the closest farm to my home, Perry Cottage. I would just walk from our cottage on Matching Green, past the village school and just a few hundred yards up Watery Lane to Waterman's End.

But if I took the other fork opposite the school towards Little Laver, I would first reach the drive to Little Laver Hall after about half a mile and if I continued straight on, I would reach Little Laver Grange after one mile.

Squire, Herman James Meyer, lived at Little Laver Grange. He was born in 1868 into a tremendously wealthy family and was the most prominent Squire in our locality. He was a portly, stockily built man with a waxed moustache and a military bearing. His voice cracked like a rifle shot and most of his sentences were punctuated by 'What!' He was rarely seen without his gun when walking around the estate, and he was always impeccably dressed in knickerbockers, stockings and brown lace-up boots.

Squire in his rose garden
Herman James Meyer,
1868 - 1945

To lace up his boots was the limit of arduous labour that Squire undertook himself. For all other tasks he had housekeeper, maid, farm hands -- and me.

"Fred," his staccato voice would rap out. The voice

76

was swiftly followed by the 'plonk, plonk' sound of a pair of wet, muddy boots landing somewhere near me. We had just returned after a day's shooting and I was busy cleaning Squire's gun. At first, the noisy appearance of the boots terrified me. Later on, it amused me. Squire's blissful unawareness of the reality that boot polish does not apply to a wet boot, should not really have been a surprise to me. Somehow though, I learned the tricks of the trade and he would invariably find a nicely polished pair of boots next morning.

Squire, like all people of his upbringing and at that time early this century, still lived in a world where servants were servants and were made to serve their masters. You walked a few paces behind and spoke only when spoken to. We all knew exactly where we stood and what our position in life was.

I loved the days when I was asked to go shooting with Squire. Heavily burdened with his gun and other tackle, I would humbly walk behind him across the fields. When in position, I loaded his gun and directed his spaniel 'Punch' to pick up the game.

The rules and paraphernalia of shooting were familiar to me. My Uncle George, who looked after game and garden for Squire, had first taken me along to shoots as a boy beater when I was seven years old. Provided I had something to wear, I would present myself to my Uncle George at Little Laver Grange at 9am on shooting Saturdays for beater duty.

My love for the shooting sport grew steadily from those early experiences as a seven year old, and I have not missed any of the next eighty-three seasons.

After I had started to work, I would still, after hours, walk over to the neighbouring Envilles estate to see the gamekeeper, Mr Humphrey. I liked helping Mr Humphrey.

Envilles
Leaves from a Hunting Diary in Essex, by H Beauchamp Yerburgh, 1900

The estate owner's three sons served in the army during the 1914-18 war and the shoot was kept going, as best as possible, to provide some recreational sport for the young officers when home on leave.

"Boy," Mr Humphrey would say, "I am going to Ongar tonight. You stay with the pheasants."

A neatly dressed Mr Humphrey would set off to walk the ten miles to Ongar and back while I spent the evening protecting the birds from vermin. Mr Humphrey walked everywhere. He did not know how to ride a bicycle. On shooting days Mr Humphrey would be outstandingly smartly dressed in his headkeeper's clothes of velveteen jacket (a bit like my unfortunate childhood jacket with three buttons at the back, but with a shorter tail), breeches, stockings and immaculate white spats.

He did not have any money to pay me for my services, but he would always give me a rabbit or two. In this way, I not only learned about the shooting field and gamekeeping, but it also provided us with a good Sunday dinner.

It is hard to imagine quite how many rabbits there were -- thousands of them. Today's farmers consider that they have a rabbit problem when they see a few. Myxomatosis largely destroyed the vast rabbit populations.

I have a lot to thank rabbits for. I most probably have to thank them for having helped me to grow into a strong, healthy, six-foot man. Granny always joked that I would have been a big fellow if I had had enough to eat when growing up. Rabbits were the mainstay of our lives, supplemented by birds -- blackbirds, thrushes, moorhens, even sparrows -- which we children would catch in a brick trap.

Squire applied for my first gun licence when I was eighteen years old and I could hardly contain myself for joy. I could never have afforded the ten bob it cost.

But first, I had to receive my shooting lesson. Uncle George asked me to come into the meadow with him.

I was proudly striding out, carrying Squire's gun, when eagle-eyed Uncle George spotted a rabbit amongst a bunch of grasses. I cocked the gun.

"Oh, no, you don't", he stopped me. "You have got to make it run."

With this he proceeded to make such a hullabaloo that the rabbit took off in fright. I took the gun up to my shoulder, took aim, most probably said a quick prayer as well, and shot the rabbit.

"Ha'," exhaled Uncle George. "That wasn't too bad, but you were a little bit behind it. Aim just over the ears."

"At least," he muttered, "it was safe."

As we walked back to the house Squire came out.

"How did you get on, Fred," demanded Squire very

'Uncle George'
George Henry Perry,
1883 - 1977

sharply, his eyes turning to interrogate my uncle.

"Not too bad, sir. He killed a rabbit," Uncle George replied.

"But was he safe," demanded Squire.

"Yes, sir, otherwise I should have brought him home."

Squire was an absolute stickler for safety in shooting and this day was my first experience of the event which would take place each and every time before I was allowed to go out with a gun. It never varied for as long as I knew H. J. Meyer. Out of the top drawer of his desk Squire took a card and I was called on to read the inscription aloud:

80

If a sportsman true you'll be,
listen carefully to me.
Never, never let your gun,
pointed be at anyone.
That it may unloaded be,
matters not the least to me.

Many years later Squire made me a present of one of his guns -- a lovely twelve bore Cogswell & Harrison hammerless, sidelock gun. Unexpectedly one day as we were returning from a day's shooting, he suddenly turned to me.

"Fred, I will give you this gun," he said abruptly while thrusting the gun into my hands. "It has never suited me very well. You shoot far better with it than I will ever."

"If I leave it to you," he added. "I know that you will never get it. I don't trust these lawyers."

"And while I think of it, I will write a note to confirm this," he said, and disappeared into his study. He had the letter signed and witnessed by the clerk of the justices and Mrs Van der Gucht, his sister - just in case anybody should ever challenge my owning such a splendid gun.

Squire had inherited the Little Laver estate in 1894 when he was twenty-six years old. His family, he told me, had originally been wealthy diamond merchants who came to England in the sixteenth century. Squire's ancestor, also called Herman Meyer, had arrived with King George I

Forty Hall, Enfield

81

[Hanovarian Accession in 1714] and was naturalised by act of parliament in 1714. The Meyers' early place of business had been Leadenhall Street in the City of London and they resided at Forty Hall in Enfield.

Forty Hall was a very substantial manor house set in three hundred acres of parkland. Squire told me, many years later, that his family had at one time been quite unable to count their wealth.

Squire's grandfather, Christian Paul Meyer, married four times and left Forty Hall in the hands of his oldest son and his family, while he came to live at Little Laver with the rest of his family. He built the manor house, now known as Little Laver Hall, on the site of a previous house, in the middle of the last century. In those years and in my early childhood, the house was known as Park Hall. The villagers set their clocks by Park Clock, the clock above the stables at the Hall. Upon his death, the estate went to Squire's father, who had four children by his first wife and none by the second, third or the fourth.

Herman Paul Meyer, Squire's father
Leaves from a Hunting Diary in Essex,
by H Beauchamp Yerburgh, 1900

My Squire, Herman James Meyer, was born in 1868 as the younger son, and lost his mother when he was only five years old. Listening to him, as I did a great deal over the years and when he was rather lonely in his old age, makes me believe that he had a very unhappy childhood, being brought up by two stepmothers. His father had not paid a lot of attention to him, possibly because he was very absorbed with his new wives; or possibly because Squire was not as good a sportsman as his brother. Squire always said that he had been a disappointment to his father. But he adored his older brother and was immensely fond of his childhood nanny, Jane Bateman.

Squire never married. He was of the opinion that almost all women were scheming hussies and that his grandfather's and father's many wives had substantially reduced the family fortune. Whilst he was always immensely courteous to the women of his acquaintance, he made it quite clear that married life was not for him.

Squire came into his inheritance when his beloved elder brother, Christian Paul, was killed in the hunting field in 1894: a small fence, a riderless horse and a man on the ground with a broken back. Many years later, I heard Doctor Shields say to Squire: "Today it would be no problem to have treated your brother and very likely he would have survived." But in those days a rider had to be dispatched for help. Eventually, a farm cart arrived and he was then jolted the many miles across rough ploughed fields to the cottage hospital. Christian Paul died the following day and his brother, Herman James Meyer, the man I have known as Squire all my life, was called home from Canada.

Squire had been totally distraught at the loss of his brother and in addition now had to face the daunting task of running the estate at Little Laver and other holdings at Stondon Massey. It was a task for which he had neither the training nor the inclination. His grief apparently was so great that he could not continue living at the family home, Park Hall [later called Little Laver Hall]. His brother, by all accounts, had been a very likeable and popular man. Everything at the family house reminded my Squire of the loss of his brother and he took the decision that life there would be unbearable for him.

His nanny, Jane Bateman, had some years earlier at the advanced age of thirty-five married the Meyers' estate bailiff, Alfred Lucking. They lived at the home farm, Little Laver Hall Farm, which is now known as Little Laver Grange. They had one son, Henry Lucking [farmer Lucking - my first employer].

Little Laver Grange & Church

It was to Little Laver Grange that Squire moved in his grief. He had the house extended and occupied his own suite of rooms in the farmhouse.

Squire's brother was buried in the vault at Little Laver churchyard. The church and graveyard lie right alongside Little Laver Grange.

One of the old stockmen at Little Laver Grange told me that his wife, who was a maid there, had to go down into the burial vault regularly and dust the coffins. I don't think it bothered her greatly. It was just part of her job.

Given the close relationship between Squire and Henry Lucking's' mother, it is not altogether surprising that in due course Henry Lucking took over when his father died and became the tenant farmer to the Meyer estate at Little Laver. He married a distant cousin -- I am quite sure to get out from under the clutches of his mother -- and lived for the rest of his life at Waterman's End.

The reason for this detailed explanation about Squire's family is to illustrate the unusual relationship between my two employers: Herman James Meyer, Esquire, and Henry Lucking, tenant farmer. Squire's tenant farmer was his nanny's son. And quite contrary to normal etiquette, Henry Lucking addressed Squire as 'Master James', which would undoubtedly have been the way his mother had addressed her charge.

Squire had been forced to take over the management of the estate by his brothers death. It had not been his wish. I don't think he ever took much pleasure in the task. He much preferred the hunting and shooting field. Mind you, after his brother's death, he never rode to hounds again; his dead brother's horse was put down, but he always remained a keen follower and supporter of the hunt.

In 1903 Squire offered the farm up for sale, but withdrew it again without having accepted any offers. I do not know the reasons for this.

PLAN № 1.

LOTS 1 & 2.

MATCHING GREEN

②

86

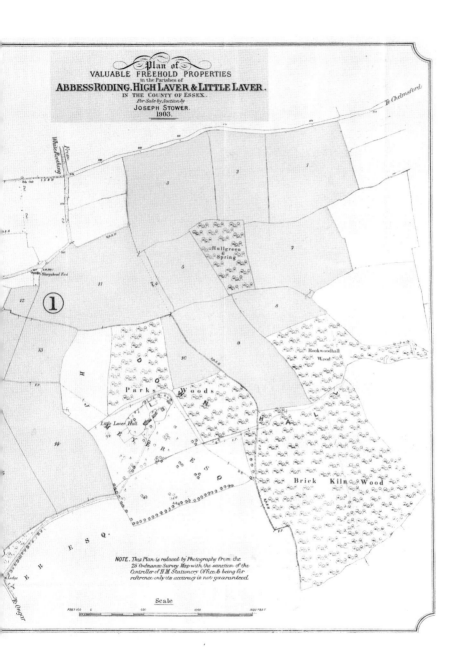

Plan of
VALUABLE FREEHOLD PROPERTIES
in the Parishes of
ABBESS RODING, HIGH LAVER & LITTLE LAVER.
IN THE COUNTY OF ESSEX.
For Sale by Auction by
JOSEPH STOWER.
1903.

NOTE. This Plan is reduced by Photography from the
25 Ordnance Survey Map with the sanction of the
Controller of H.M. Stationery Office & being for
reference only its accuracy is not guaranteed.

Scale

Lot 2.

(Coloured PINK on Plan No. 1.)

THE ADJOINING

FREEHOLD PROPERTY,

OF ABOUT

86 a. : 1 r. : 25 p.,

KNOWN AS

WATERMAN'S END FARM,

In the Parishes of HIGH LAVER and LITTLE LAVER,

situate close to the picturesque Essex Village of Matching Green, about 6 miles from Ongar, and about 5 from Harlow and 9 miles respectively from the Market Towns of Epping and Bishops Stortford. It comprises

AN ATTRACTIVE RESIDENCE,

with tiled roof, approached from the road by a Carriage Sweep Drive, and containing—

Three good Upper Bed Rooms, and a smaller one, DINING ROOM fitted with slow combustion grate, DRAWING ROOM adjoining, another small Sitting Room next the Front Entrance, Dairy, Kitchen, Lumber Room, and small Store Room, Outside w.c.

FRONT LAWN AND CAPITAL KITCHEN GARDEN,

and in Outer Yard—Boot-house, timber and tiled Brew-house, a range of timber and tiled Buildings of Gig-house, Poultry-house, Meal-house and Piggery.

AMPLE FARM PREMISES,

including timber and thatched Barn and lean-to Nag Stable, timber and tiled Hen-house, Cow-house, thatched Cart-horse Stable for 3 horses, Open Cattle Sheds with slated roofs, another large timber and thatched Barn with Cart Shed adjoining, spacious Stock Yards next road, and a

TIMBER, PLASTER AND TILED DOUBLE TENEMENT AND GARDEN

together with the several Enclosures of

1903

88

ARABLE AND PASTURE LANDS,

partly bounded and intersected by a Stream and divided as follows :—

No. on Plan.	Description.	Cultivation.	A.	R.	P.
	IN THE PARISH OF HIGH LAVER.				
1A	Hull Green Field (part of)	Arable	0	3	11
34	Little Perry Field	Ditto	5	0	9
41	Great Perry Field	Ditto	3	2	37
46	Matching Green Field	Ditto	5	1	26
47	Cart Shed Field	Ditto }	16	2	30
48	Hulks Field	Ditto }			
50	Longs Downs	Ditto	4	2	5
				36	0	38
	IN THE PARISH OF LITTLE LAVER.				
6A	Hull Green Field (part of)	Arable	7	1	15
8A	Kitchen Field	Ditto	6	2	38
9A	Residence, Garden, Farm Premises, Yards and Cottage	....	0	3	19
10A	New Leys	Meadow }	8	2	2
11A	Pump Meadow	Ditto }			
22A	Daniels Mead	Ditto	3	1	35
26	Mill Field	Arable	8	1	16
111	Mill Hoppitt	Arable	14	3	22
				50	0	27

Total Acres......86 1 25

Let to Mr. ALFRED LUCKING, on the terms of an Agreement for a Yearly Tenancy, from Michaelmas, 1889, at the Rent of £66 per Annum.

The Tenant covenants to pay all Rates, Taxes and other Outgoings (except Landlord's Property Tax), also all Tithe and Tithe Rent Charge, which for the half-year ending the 1st October, 1902, amounted to £5 12s. 9d. in respect of the Lands in Little Laver Parish, and £4 7s. 4d. for the same period for Lands in the Parish of High Laver.

This Lot is believed to be free of Land Tax.

On the whole, Squire left the farming to his tenants, who were not always as scrupulous in paying their rent as they should have been.

This particularly applied to Henry Lucking. But I did not know this until many years later.

I think Squire felt thoroughly uncomfortable in the position in which he had been inadvertently put, with his tenant farmer also being his old nanny's son. This unusual relationship caused Squire much trouble over the years. I don't think he ever felt that he could treat him as he might have treated any other erring tenant farmer in that any tough action might have resulted in hurting 'Nanny'.

That set the scene for all the years to come -- in effect the years I worked for Mr Lucking and Squire.

As Squire got older, he came to trust and rely on me somewhat more, and he would sometimes speak to me about it. His solicitor, Mr Dan Harrison of Collier Bristow, London, who was also his cousin, was invariably very annoyed that Squire would never take the action he had advocated, such as showing Henry Lucking the door for non payment of rent.

But as Squire said to me one evening late in his life: "I could never do it. I could never take the legal action I should have taken. After all, he was Nanny's son." He showed me a letter from the solicitor which pointed out in no uncertain terms that by writing off the rent owed to him by Henry Lucking he had in effect just made Mr Lucking a gift of two thousand pounds.

Squire was in such a state that he asked me to read the letter to him. I recall very little of the wording except the sum of two thousand pounds and the advice that it was time to take some very firm action. "How can I?" Squire shrugged resignedly. "I know I should be firmer with him, but how can I? It would only upset Nanny."

Two thousand pounds in the late 1920s was an awful lot of money. I have worked out that with my pay at the time, it

90

would have taken me twenty years to earn that amount. In those days, one could buy a very nice cottage on the Green for fifty pounds; a cottage that would fetch two hundred thousand pounds in today's market.

At some point, Squire told me that he was paying more in tithe to the church than he was receiving in rent from his tenant farmer, Henry Lucking.

I am not sure, but possibly because I liked the fun-loving Henry Lucking so much despite his meanness, I may have drawn a picture in my mind blaming his wife for being the tight-fisted one. She gave him an awfully hard time sometimes and would begrudge me any extra penny I may have earned.

Chapter 7

"Fred," Squire barked, "I shall need you on Saturday."
He had been invited by Major Hoare to shoot at the
neighbouring estate, Envilles. "You won't have to do anything
but look after me," Squire said.

Saturday arrived, damp and windy. I got thoroughly
drenched on my way to pick up Punch, Squire's spaniel, before
making my way to the meeting point at Red House farm. I was
not exactly in the best of temper on my arrival. My mood did
not improve when Major Maitland Tower, a rather mildewed
old gentleman approached us.

"Gad, Meyer," he wheezed, "might your chap look after
me as well?"

"Right ho," Squire replied, "Fred, you look after the
Major too."

William Maitland Tower
(in younger days)
Leaves from a Hunting Diary in Essex,
by H Beauchamp Yerburgh, 1900

I squelched my miserable way
from drive to drive. Through
woods and over muddy,
ploughed fields I trudged,
weighed down by two pairs of
waders, mackintoshes, two guns,
cartridge cases and shooting
sticks. My feet had trebled in
size with huge clumps of heavy
mud, making it difficult not to
stumble over Punch who
blissfully scampered around me.
At each drive, I would first
deposit Squire and his kit, then
take the old major to his gun
position.

Eventually we finished the last wretched drive.

"I say," the old major piped, "I got a partridge up, and I know damn well it's dead."

Dumping his tackle right there and then in the middle of the meadow, Squire briefly glanced up at me, then said, "Fred, go look for the Major's bird."

Still lumbered with the major's kit, his waders hanging from my shoulders and knocking against the back of my legs, Punch and I set off in search of the elusive partridge. The weather got even thicker, but finally I was able to present the major with his bird. "Good man," he acknowledged.

"I can go home from here," he said. "If you just come with me to that corner over there, I can manage the last bit on my own." I duly took him that extra mile.

Having arrived at the corner, the old fossil fumbled in his pocket, muttering, "You have been of great help to me today." This was highly encouraging -- possibly I might be able to afford a few cigarettes. In those days, I still smoked. Out came the hand -- holding a miserly sixpence.

I put on a passable show of being grateful and made my way back to the meadow.

Having picked up Squire's abandoned tackle, Punch and I made our weary way through puddles and over sodden ground back to Little Laver Grange.

"Did you find the bird?" Squire asked.

"Yes, sir, we found a partridge. Whether it was the major's bird I don't know," I said. By now, I was old enough to have acquired a certain amount of cheek. "And I took him practically to his door."

"I am sure you were well rewarded," Squire countered.

"Thank you, sir, I got sixpence."

Squire threw back his head and fair roared with laughter. Then he took out his wallet and gave me a ten shilling note as a reward.

On another occasion, Squire was invited to shoot as a guest of Mr Baron at White Roding. The High Sheriff of Hampshire and Loftus Arkwright, who owned much of the land on which now stands Harlow New Town, were also guests at the shoot.

The morning had been a disaster. No sport at all! Few feathers to be seen!

This was a matter of some concern to Mr Baron, given the importance of the guests. What also mattered was that Mr Baron was not a very popular man in the village. He was a wealthy stockbroker and a bit of a bully -- well, he was a bully.

On this shoot, though, the bully had his comeuppance. He had invited all these toffs and only one or two birds had obliged his guests. Oh, was he angry!

Squire had accepted the invitation, but in truth had little time for the man. He was civil enough to him -- but he didn't like the way Baron treated people.

"Fred, this morning has been a washout, what!" Squire boomed to me at lunchtime. "Baron is a bit annoyed. Do you think we could arrange for a few drives on my land? Call your Uncle George out."

Honour was at stake and we chose our drives with care. The place had not been shot hard for years. Squire never asked more than five friendly guns -- hardly a really good shot amongst them. Normally, if they managed to bag 25 partridges between them, they would have missed at least 50. The place was teeming with partridges.

Blimey, Baron and his guests had a hell of a good afternoon! I'll never forget the last drive -- a field with low-growing sugar beet. We managed to break up the birds. They rose high and fast, wings beating like rolls on drums, in ones and twos instead of bunching together. They had to lift above a tall old hedge, everyone of them a challenge. The birds fair whistled overhead. By golly, we saw some shooting that afternoon -- absolutely wonderful.

At the end, I remember going over to Loftus Arkwright. He was very wealthy and said to be amongst the best six shots in England. But for all that he looked like a little old wizened chimney sweep with an old handkerchief around his neck. Still, he had presence and -- oh my, could he shoot! My admiration must have shown, because he cocked a bushy eyebrow at me and said, "Doesn't matter how good you are -- there's always one that beats you."

I asked him whether he wanted a dog -- just in case he had one or two wounded birds on the ground. "Don't think so," he answered, "I have got 11 down and they are all dead. Though I did enjoy the ones that got away." He had a proper sporting spirit.

At the end of the afternoon's shooting, the High Sheriff of Hampshire gave me a half a pound. Loftus Arkwright gave me a pound. The other guns were very grateful too.

When as usual at the end of the day I reported to Squire, he said,

"Well done. We showed them something." Honour had been satisfied. Squire had the satisfaction of showing Baron's guests some decent sport. To be honest, we had also put one across the bully.

Squire was in very fine humour and brought out a bottle of port to celebrate this very satisfying afternoon. Then he did something I have never seen done again: he took his sword, bottle of port in the other hand and with one swift movement lobbed the cork complete with bottleneck clean off. Sounds like stuff out of Musketeer movies, but I saw him do it right there in front of me.

"I don't like to ask you, Fred, but how did you get on?" Squire enquired.

"Well, sir, I have never known anything like it -- I picked up five pounds."

He responded with delight: "Fred, I'll double it." And he did.

At the end of the day, he concluded, "I won't have them come here again!"

I, of course, wished fervently that they -- and another ten pounds -- would. To me it was an awful lot of money -- the equivalent of six to seven weeks' wages. I put my windfall straight into my Post Office savings account.

The following week, I had two jobs offered to me. One of the guns at the shoot said to me: "Perry, if you are ever looking for a job, please come and see me first." But to top it all, Baron sent his manservant with a note ordering me to come and see him. He was most put out when I did not accept his job offer. Imagine, the man had been Squire's guest and there he was committing the ultimate sin of trying to poach one of his host's servants. That sort of thing just isn't done, and I was happy enough where I was.

Squire, in his own way, was a very caring person. It was part of my job each morning to walk to Butt Hatch wood to check on the coops where young, motherless pheasants were being raised. In those far off days, nobody bought in birds as they do today, we looked after our existing stock. To reach the wood entailed a three to four mile walk each way, before I even started my regular morning routine of filling the coal scuttles and emptying the rubbish pails at Squire's house.

Meanwhile Squire would be having his breakfast. Right on the dot of nine o'clock -- he was very strict about time-keeping -- he would come over to instruct me on today's tasks.

"Look sharp, Perry," he commanded on this occasion. "We are going over to the wood." It was obviously his intention to have a look at what was going on in the wood himself, and my feet had not even dried yet from my earlier walk there. You see, in the early morning, regardless of the weather, the fields were always wet from mist, dew or rain. The headlands were not sprayed against weed growth as they are today. Apart from the fact that the chemicals were not available, it was in the headlands that most birds nested. Hence we would walk through the tall and wet corn, taking care not to damage too many ears of corn as we went.

Squire strode ahead and I would follow three paces behind. On our way back from the wood, Squire noticed that I was lagging a little further behind than the customary pace. I was having some difficulty keeping up with him as my feet were in a very sorry state. My boots and stockings were soaking wet and my knickerbockers were clinging damply to my knees. By this time, mid morning, I had already walked fifteen to twenty miles in quite inadequate footwear. My boots were certainly not watertight and my teenage feet had most probably outgrown them as well.

"Perry, you know how to ride my bicycle, what!" Squire said to me as we reached Little Laver Grange. "This afternoon I want you to go to Ongar for me. I have a few errands I want you to undertake and I also want you to take a note to Mr Tadgell."

I was delighted. To be allowed to ride Squire's bicycle was a real treat -- and would give my feet a break too. I rode the five miles to Ongar, completed the shopping for Squire and called on Mr Tadgell to give him Squire's note.

Ongar
Leaves from a Hunting Diary in Essex, by H Beauchamp Yerburgh, 1900

"Oh dear," Mr Tadgell said, "I can see what Squire means. Your poor feet." Mr Tadgell was the manager of Ashdowns, the smart men's outfitters.

"Sit yourself down and take those boots off," he said. "Here is a cloth. Do dry your feet and we will see if we can fit you a decent pair of boots."

"But first," Mr Tadgell said, and he opened a drawer in the counter. "There, these will keep you warm," and he passed me a pair of lovely thick woollen stockings to put on.

"I know what life is like on Matching Green," he continued sympathetically. "I have relatives living there. I don't think Squire will mind one bit if I give you two pair of these stockings." He had clearly guessed that I did not have another pair to change into.

It was heaven to pull on the lovely dry stockings and then Mr Tadgell fitted me with the most wonderful pair of well-made boots.

"Comfortable?" he enquired. "That's all right then."

Dear me, what a wonderful pair of boots. My feet felt so snug in them. I thought I had gone to heaven. I was so elated that I can recall little of the ride home, but as usual Squire did not want any thanks. He was very gruff when I tried to thank him.

He was a very respected man. The shopkeepers and merchants of Ongar, I am sure, would gladly have sent the entire contents of their shops to him, had he sent a note to that effect. Most probably Squire settled the account for my lovely boots and stockings when he was in Ongar next; which was quite often as he sat as a magistrate in the Ongar court and had a seat on the Ongar rural district council.

In later years, Squire would often give me the task of finding out who of the parishioners was in need. He rather felt that the gentry had not always looked after the workers and their families very well.

Discretion was the essence of this mission. Squire did not want it to be known that he was helping out. For instance, when I found somebody in dire straits for a pair of boots for a child, Squire would instruct me to send them to Silcocks -- the saddlers on Matching Green. There the needy person would be fitted with a new pair of boots.

I am quite sure the beneficiaries all knew who was paying for these unexplained 'God sends', but under no circumstances did Squire want acknowledgement -- or pray, even thanks. He hated people being 'grateful' to him.

I recall him being very angry when he received a letter from his tenant thanking him for repairs to his cottage, the Leather Bottle. The letter closed: "I remain, sir, yours humbly." Oh dear, I have rarely seen Squire so cross: "Don't ever say that. There is no need to humble yourself, I need you most probably more than you need me."

I often think of Squire as I stroll along the lanes. His sense of equality did not extend to my walking alongside him rather than behind, or to speaking when not spoken to.

Yet, Squire was a very kind man, particularly in his later years, when he had recognised that most parishioners in Little Laver and Matching Green were leading an incredibly hard life.

Given the constraints of the period and his class, he tried very hard to consider us as human beings of equal worth. I reckon, if he lived today, he would be a considered a liberal.

Chapter 8

When I was fifteen years old I achieved one of my major ambitions -- I joined the cricket club.

My friends and I usually played cricket with homemade bats, on dirt paths or in our yard. The cricket club itself, even though only two hundred yards away in the middle of the Green, belonged to a different world -- the world of squires, farmers and gentlemen, not boys who worked on the land.

Mr Gingell, the farmer from High Laver Grange, and Mr Reeves, a stockbroker, were observing us as we were 'practising' on a rough patch of grass towards the edge of the Green.

"Why don't you give these boys a game? Some of them are quite good, you know," Basil Gingell remarked. Mr Reeves eyed us coldly, drew himself up in a manner that resembled a cockerel in full crow, and squawked: "Can't play them! They're not members -- and never will be!"

Mr Gingell at first looked incredulously at Mr Reeves and then asked him rather angrily: "How on earth could they become members?" Basil Gingell, who knew of the realities of our lives, turned to me:

"How much money do you have in your pocket, Perry? How much pocket money do you get?"

"Sixpence, sir," I replied, standing to attention with my cap in hand. Gingell turned round furiously and faced Reeves:

"What t'hell do you know about anything? Well they are members now!" He whipped his wallet out of his pocket and handed the astonished Reeves ten shillings -- our membership fee of half a crown for each boy. Reeves, seething with indignation, looked at us with the expression of somebody who has just smelt a rotten fish, but finally managed only a feeble "Right ho".

I played cricket for the club on the very next Saturday -- a boy playing in a men's eleven. I made seven runs not out and I held a catch. Afterwards, I remember standing in front of the pavilion and Basil Gingell ruffled my hair in a gruff, yet affectionate way, saying, "You'll make a cricketer, boy."

Henry Lucking, Squire's tenant farmer who I worked for, loved my 'joining' the cricket club. One very cold day in June, he was scheduled to umpire our game. Whenever Lucking umpired, however, the game was more a pantomime than a serious game of cricket. The opposition was never in two minds about Henry Lucking. They either loved him, or they hated him. He would make fun of everything right from the word go.

" Where is your sweater, Freddie John?" Henry Lucking boomed as he saw rubbing my arms trying to keep warm. He always called me Freddie John.

"I ain't got one, sir," I replied.

He looked around. "Has anybody got a bicycle?" he enquired. "Go to Waterman's End, see the missus and tell her to send my cricket sweater. Tell her, she'll find it in my tie box."

The sweater duly arrived and I pulled it over my head. My small frame was totally swamped by the huge man's sweater. I rolled the sleeves up as best I could and sat down on a hen coop on the edge of the cricket ground watching the game and awaiting my turn.

My time came to go in to bat. The bowler ran at me and quite unruffled by the presence of more seasoned performers I hit the ball -- I was used to playing on rough footpaths and this lovely wicket did not frighten me a bit. I ran up the wicket. I did it two or three times, but I may have gone too far for the opposition appealed to the umpire for a run-out. Henry

Lucking looked a little taken aback for a moment and then he grinned at them: "I don't know, he's turned round inside his bloody sweater and I don't know whether he's coming or going."

Henry Lucking's antics did not always please Squire very much. He liked him well enough, but had little stomach for his pranks. But they endeared him greatly to me. I found Mr Lucking tremendous fun and I was enormously fond of him. He was always laughing. Always up to some mischief and he took a genuine if childish pleasure in it.

Squire was pleased that I had taken to cricket: "Good character-forming sport, what!"

He promised to buy me a pair of white flannels if I was picked to play for Matching Green. Hence, when I was sixteen years old, before my first match in the first eleven, I was able to cycle to Ongar and, yet again with a note from Squire addressed to Mr Tadgell, acquired a pair of brand new, well-fitting cricket flannels. Now, I owned a better pair of flannels than anybody, and my mother, who was home on her annual holiday, bought me a decent shirt to go with it. Thus, properly kitted out, I was ready for action.

I was ever so fussy over my beautiful new kit, but every time we played in away matches there was another hurdle to overcome -- transport. This was provided by a Matching man, Stanley Owers, who had started a little haulage and coal business after he was demobbed after the war, but his van was always covered in coal dust and you had to be very careful where you sat. It was no mean feat to arrive at the host club in the same pristine condition as when we set out from Matching Green. After all, being turned out well is important. Also, there might be a couple of girls there to chat up after the match.

Clogham's Green, a village five miles from Matching Green, was one of Squire's favourite cricket grounds. He loved it, with its thatched cricket pavilion surrounded by fields and woods. A little, crooked cottage overlooked the Green and always reminded me of the story of the lady who lived in a shoe: little children running in and out all the time.

The cricket facilities were good, and included the adjacent King William pub. It was at this venue that Squire decided one year to hold a friendly match.

At the last minute one of the players in his team had let him down due to illness and Squire had to ask Henry Lucking to step in.

"Henry, none of your parodies on this occasion. I want you to go in batting. Just do your best and stay there as long as you can," he counselled.

Henry Lucking gave him a big grin and got himself in position. The parson from High Easter, who was bowling, came running up the wicket, when Henry Lucking raised a hefty hand, stopping him. "I am sorry, I have got something in my eye which will have to be removed." He took out his handkerchief and fiddled with his eye for a few minutes. "Ah, that's better."

The parson strolled back and started to run in again. Up came Lucking's big hand again. "Have to adjust my attire," he said, and proceeded to buckle up his pads.

The parson, somewhat miffed by this time, walked back again and made another start. Lucking put his hand up once more. "Stop, stop," he cried. "It is always my custom to say good morning to my opponents," he said, stretching out his large hand.

The parson allowed Henry Lucking to pump his hand, but looked like thunder. "I should think that now you will let me play cricket," he hissed, and with the next ball he bowled Lucking out.

"What do you think you were doing, Henry?" Squire accosted Lucking angrily as he came off the field.

"Well, you said I should stay there as long as possible and I couldn't think of a better way," Mr Lucking smirked. "If I could have, I would have stopped him again. Surely that is as good as four balls."

The time came for the opposition to bat. The captain had asked Mr Lucking to be the opening bowler. Squire was huffing and puffing over this, but couldn't do anything about it -- it was the captain's choice.

Henry Lucking walked back. In fact, he walked right off the Green. He opened the field gate and walked all the way out to the woods. "You'll know when I'm coming back, because the rooks will start to fly," he shouted and walked on until the only sight of him was his bald head bobbing along the edge of the wood. By this time, everybody who knew Henry Lucking was smiling in anticipation.

Finally, he turned and walked back along the woods on to the cricket ground. Here he did a little jig, hopped and skipped, and danced a few more steps. Then he proceeded to tear up the wicket, stopped dead and bowled a slowly dropping lob. By this time the batsman was laughing so much that he missed the ball altogether -- and lost his wicket.

The farmers met frequently at Silcocks, the saddlers, to hold inquests on cricket matches. Silcocks was right next door to the post office shop facing the Green and was the farmers' main gossip shop.

Occasionally a farmhand would come in to buy a harness: they would greet the farmers respectfully and leave again as quickly as possible. Farmhands were not encouraged to linger at Silcocks, for this was farmers' territory.

Having the shop clogged up with farmers did not always please the saddlers very much, as they found it difficult to get on with their work. On the other hand, they could not upset their customers. A bench ran right round the room displaying the saddlery and boots for sale. On one side of the saddlers' room worked Monty Silcock, the stitcher, and on the other side his brother Percy, the saddler who did the hammering.

As usual, the saddler's shop was blue with pipe smoke, and the strategy for a forthcoming event was being planned: the annual 'President's eleven' match. This was going to be a very important game. The great cricketer Canon Gillingham, an Essex opening batsman, and two distinguished MCC members would be playing. Gillingham's highest score had been 209, for Essex against Middlesex, and he was going to be a formidable opponent. But we had beaten him before and it was the two others which bothered us more.

Bill Furze, the farmer from Hull Green, was going to bowl and was rather concerned about the opposition. Chewing his pipe, his brow wrinkled as he addressed Henry Lucking: "They're out of our league. We can't beat them."

"Not so bloody much of that," Henry Lucking replied. "We'll give them a match, neighbour."

"Do stop that racket you are making with your hammer for a moment," Mr Lucking shouted across to Silcock. "I can't hear a thing over that din.

Turning back to Bill Furze, he said: "You'll see. Never mind where the ball goes, you appeal."

"Remember, neighbour, I'll be umpiring," he added meaningfully.

The great day arrived. Both MCC members were out in no time. Bill Furze had bowled, appealed with a "how's that?", and on each occasion Mr Lucking had popped his pipe up and the batsmen were ruled out. I was fielding and couldn't believe my eyes.

What could the opposition do? To argue with the umpire was simply not done, and two jolly good players were out. Canon Gillingham, the Essex batsman, walked over to Henry Lucking and enquired: "Where did you learn the laws of cricket?"

"Laws of cricket?" Mr Lucking looked a bit baffled for a moment and then his face widened into a broad smile: "Reverend, I know nothing about the laws of cricket, but I make umpiring my speciality."

Oh dear, the villagers laughed about it for months. In latter years, when I had become captain of the cricket club, Squire always told me: "For God's sake, don't let Lucking umpire. He'll make a mockery of the game." Squire was terrified of Mr Lucking's umpiring. But Mr Lucking loved cricket, and his wife was happy to let him play. While he was playing cricket, he could not get up to any other capers she might disapprove of. And the villagers all loved Henry Lucking for his fooling around. They didn't care tuppence that it 'might bring the game into disrepute.'

While he loved all sports, Henry Lucking was not a very good shot and he didn't mind admitting it. I remember him telling me on one occasion: "Freddie John, I took my gun down to the spinney. There are too many rooks about and they are after the newly drilled corn."

"Imagine," he continued, "when I got near, there were a few pheasants sitting on the gate. Ah, I thought, there's my chance for some Sunday dinner. I pulled the trigger. Bang! And away the buggers flew."

On another occasion Mr Lucking was shooting with Mr Whitehead at White Roding. I was there as a beater, as usual.

As was common practice, whenever a partridge nest had been disturbed, the eggs would be gathered in and hatched under a broody hen. Eventually these partridges would be released again in the hope that they would adjust to living in the wild. Quite often, however, these birds would not become good flyers. In the manner of hens they would fly a little, then run, fly a little and then run again. It was such a clutch of partridge that Mr Lucking came upon.

After the drive, he walked back towards us looking very pleased with himself. "There you are," he said, holding up his trophy, "that's my contribution."

"Look," Mr Whitehead called out, "Lucking has got a brace of partridge." He hesitated and then said: "I bet you shot them running."

"That's where you have made a bloody mistake," Mr Lucking unashamedly retorted. "I waited till they stopped."

He wasn't a bit embarrassed at his unsportsmanlike behaviour and they loved having him along. The whole shooting party would be entertained by his jokes during lunch.

Once he did actually shoot a partridge in the orthodox manner.

"Excellent shot, Mr Lucking," exclaimed the gamekeeper who knew Lucking to be poor gun. "We could see it clearly from here. How much lead did you give the bird?"

"I didn't give it any bloody lead," Lucking replied. "You blew the whistle, I put my gun up and fired. The bird just about got there in time."

Mr Lucking never minded if the joke was at his expense, and he was never short of a quip. A neighbouring gentleman, Mr Bovill, had entered one of his horses in the local point-to-point race.

"I hear Bovill is putting one of his horses in the race," Lucking said to Squire. "I'll put a quid on it. Don't suppose it'll win. I believe it will be so far behind that it will have an excellent view of the race."

And he was not far out.

Chapter 9

Mrs Lucking was a stern woman. She always struck me as being a strange choice for such a jovial man as Henry Lucking. But as she was away visiting her family, there was nothing on this occasion to stop him accepting an invitation to a shoot from an old neighbour, Mr Thurgood. It might have been a different story if Mrs Lucking had been at home: she did not hold with her husband attending shooting parties -- particularly at Teddy Thurgood's.

Mr Thurgood had, some years previously, been a neighbour to Squire. He had lived at Rookwood Hall and also farmed Hull Green, Stock Hall and Moat Hall. But he had fallen out with the landlord, Mrs Calverley of Down Hall. His land bordered all the Down Hall woods and Teddy Thurgood had suffered a major rabbit problem. He was not prepared to pay rent on land where the crop was largely eaten by Down Hall rabbits.

He had married a very wealthy woman somewhat older than himself and, not being short of money, he had left the parish and bought Diggin's Farm at Willingale, a few miles away. I was not quite sure why Mrs Lucking took such exception to Mr Thurgood. Squire had told me Thurgood's entertainment had always been lavish when he lived locally. He had also ridden well to hounds and was a good tennis player, Squire said, nodding his approval.

Yet, I had heard from old farmhands that Mr Thurgood had a reputation of being a bit of an eccentric. He chose to run his farm just as he thought fit, which turned out to be in a most unorthodox and muddled manner.

On the morning of the shoot, I arrived early at Waterman's End as instructed. It was a cold but lovely, bright

January day and I started by leading the pony out of its box. It munched the apple I produced from my pocket, snorted as if pleased at the prospect of an outing and gave me no trouble when I harnessed it to the wagonette.

"Fine morning, Freddie John," Mr Lucking called across to me, "couldn't have asked for better." He was plainly in a spunky mood and looked forward to a good day's sport. We drove the short distance to Little Laver Grange to pick up Punch, the spaniel, then continued on to Diggin's Farm at Willingale.

Though I had never been to Willingale, I had heard of this small village with two churches standing right next to each other in the church yard, representing two parishes and having two vicars.

Willingale Spain & Willingale Doe
Leaves from a Hunting Diary in Essex, by H Beauchamp Yerburgh, 1900

Legend has it that they were built by two sisters who had quarrelled and each had built a church to outdo the other. I learned later that local historians believe this version of events unlikely on the grounds that one church was constructed in the twelfth century and the other in the fourteenth. But could it not be possible that the sisters lived in the fourteenth century, quarrelled and one of them built the second church right next door to the 'old' church? Whatever it was that caused these two churches to stand cheek by jowl on the same piece of ground, my preference is for the story of the two quarrelling sisters.

As we arrived at Diggin's farm, Mr Thurgood walked across to meet us. "Morning, old cock," he greeted Henry Lucking.

He was a slight man with hunched shoulders and he spoke in a highly educated, slightly nasal, voice. I was fascinated by his manner of walking -- like a pigeon, in tiny steps with toes pointed inwards, his upper body moving in short jerky actions.

But my attention, as was everybody else's, was drawn to a fox sitting in a loosebox and calmly observing our arrival.

"That's Emma, I think," said Mr Thurgood to the assembled group of men.

One of the men asked Mr Thurgood incredulously: "Aren't you going to do anything about that fox?"

"Why? Is she hungry?" Thurgood asked, and with that he walked a few steps across the yard. "Chuck, chuck," he clucked, took a handful of grain from a bin and scattered it around him. Hens came running from all corners of the yard and jostled around his feet picking up the corn. He then lifted his stick and 'crack!' knocked one hen over the head with it. He picked it up and walked back.

"Here you are, Emma old girl," he said, casually throwing the bird to the fox.

He had found the fox as a cub and put her in a loose box

where she grew up. Kill it? Absolutely not! He was definitely not going to be told by anybody what to do.

One of the fields at Diggin's was named 'All Corn' and the barley was still standing in January. In another field called 'Dreams', he had left fifteen acres of linseed, all of it good cover crop providing a haven for pheasants, rabbits and foxes. On this shoot, even though neither Mr Lucking nor Mr Thurgood were good shots, they managed to shoot forty pheasants between them. There were simply masses of birds around. They thrived at Diggin's.

"Henry, old cock," Mr Thurgood said to Mr Lucking after the last drive, "come into the house and have some port."

"You, boy," he pointed at me. "You go to the kitchen. My cook will look after you."

I needed no further prompting; a warm farmhouse kitchen was just what a cold and hungry boy needed. The cook, Emily Johnston, prepared a lovely tea for me. What a treat! I remember Miss Johnston with great fondness.

When I had eaten my meal and was warm again, I grew somewhat fidgety and joined the other farmhands in the wash-house. For our entertainment we loaded catapults with potatoes and shot rats running along the beams. We all knew that there was no need to hurry. Our masters would not reappear until well into the evening.

We were alerted by the loud hubbub of intoxicated goodbyes, noisy thanks and assurances of what a wonderful day it had been. This was the time for me to rush out and hitch up the pony. First, though, I had to expel the posse of hens which had gone to roost in our wagonette.

Mr Lucking was in excellent voice as he staggered across the farm yard, settled into his seat and broke into song:

113

"His Lordship's great fines we must pay,
if a summons we do not obey,
but it's a very fine sport,
so we close up the court,
and we all go a-hunting today."

The wagonette jolted down Diggin's drive under Henry Lucking's erratic guidance. Potholes, at the best of times, were hard to avoid in the pitch dark of night and it soon became evident that my expulsion of the hens had not been thorough enough. 'Squawk, squawk' -- a clucking, flapping cockerel had been shaken awake under my seat and was fighting as best he could to get out from between my legs.

"Chuck the bloody thing out," Henry Lucking said, his big hand disappearing beneath the seat. He grabbed the cockerel, accompanied by loud noises of protestation from the indignant and frightened bird, and flung it out with a flourish. "Let it find its own way home," Mr Lucking bellowed, straightened his coat and settled back in the seat. Waving the horse whip like a baton he recommenced his riotous singing:

"Then spoke the breezy porter,
with face as bold as brass,
I don't like your Christmas pudding,
you can stick it up your arse."

Accompanied by Mr Lucking's boisterous singing we bumped home to Waterman's End. At last I understood: this was most probably the reason why Mrs Lucking discouraged her husband's attendance at shooting parties. That Henry Lucking had had a good time could not have been a secret to anybody between Diggin's Farm and Waterman's End.

In subsequent years, I came several times to Diggin's Farm and I always enjoyed it. I had wonderful times there. I received five bob at the end of a shooting day, always a wonderful meal and a couple of rabbits to take home to Granny.

Mr Thurgood did not take advice from anybody. He was a law unto himself and he strongly objected to anybody trying to tell him what to do. On one occasion his neighbour passed Mr Thurgood as he and his men were getting ready to cut the corn.

"I am pleased you are cutting down that corn. It's about time," he commented.

Thurgood immediately turned round and instructed Tush, his horsekeeper: "Take those horses back, Tush."

"If my corn is in your way," he said, addressing his neighbour, "I'll make sure that it'll still be here this evening."

On a different occasion, Tush approached Mr Thurgood and suggested that the shed at Dukes Farm, where the horses were kept, should be cleaned out. The dung and straw had accumulated and raised the floor level by a couple of feet.

"The litter is so deep, the horses can't stand upright any longer," he horsekeeper complained to Thurgood.

"In that case, take the bloody tiles off the roof," Thurgood rebuffed him. "Let their heads come out. That way they can stand upright."

For some time after that we could see the horses' heads stick through the roof of their shed.

Similarly, he gave old Tush a hard time over a bull.

"Sorry sir," Tush said. "I can't feed him! I can't get near him! He is one hell of an angry bull."

"All right then, Tush," came the slow, nasal reply. "Start the old tractor up, load it with a bag of food and bring my gun."

Mr Thurgood, accompanied by Tush, drove the tractor to the bull's meadow.

"Open the gate, Tush," he ordered, himself remaining firmly seated on the tractor. As soon as the vehicle entered the meadow, the bull, true to his reputation, charged. It roared and careered around the meadow. Thurgood drove round and waited patiently until he had a fine rear view of the bull, and then 'bang, bang', emptied both barrels into his backside.

"A huge roar. Dung flew everywhere and the bull tore through the hedge and ran like hell, still pursued by Thurgood on his tractor. When the bull had eventually put some distance between them, Mr Thurgood calmly turned the tractor round and drove back to the gate where Tush was waiting.

"There you are, Tush. That will teach him a lesson," he said.

"Yes sir," replied Tush. "But you could hardly have expected me to shoot your bull."

I would not have liked to have worked for Mr Thurgood, but Tush could handle him well and, I think, eventually always got his way. Tush lived in a cottage on the Diggin's estate.

"Another wet place in my roof, sir," Tush said to Mr Thurgood.

"Well, haven't you got another bath to put under it?" Thurgood asked impatiently.

Eventually, of course, he would have the roof mended, but he was not going to be told by anybody how and when. Tush knew this and didn't mind. Thurgood just had to have a game with everybody.

Just in the same way he would not accept that his 'bridge' over Fyfield river was not altogether safe.

His land lay both sides of the river and the best shooting was on the far side. You could almost see his glee as he tried to lead the shooting party over what was after all only a round pole and a bind of string.

Being pigeon-toed it was quite easy for him to get across. He moved just like a cat as the pole went up and down as he stepped on it. Lucking, equally daring, charged after him with sheer foolish courage. The rest of the guns, Squire included, refused. Most were portly gentlemen and certainly not nimble enough to make it across safely. They walked miles round to be able to rejoin the shoot.

"Thurgood," Squire said. "That bridge is really not safe. You ought to have it seen to, what!"

"And who would pay for that?" Thurgood retorted.

The following week, four workmen in white coats and aprons arrived and fitted a lovely wooden bridge with a sturdy hand rail. They had partly pre-made it in their workshop and made a lovely job of erecting it over the river. The bridge had a span of about fifteen yards and was painted gleaming white. Mr Clarke, a dog biscuit manufacturer from Loughton, who was one of the guns, had ordered it to be fitted.

When Thurgood heard about this he called 'Fuzzy Day', one of his men, and Tush.

"Bring some saws and come with me," he ordered.

Under Thurgood's supervision, they sawed the bridge down.

"What do we do with it now, sir?" Fuzzy Day asked.

"Throw it in that bloody river," Thurgood replied.

"Nobody gives orders on my land except me," he added as he turned and walked away.

The wonderful bridge floated down the river in pieces and Mr Clarke was never invited to Diggin's again.

I am quite sure that Thurgood drove all the parsons away from Willingale. He had so much land that he totally dominated the parish. He simply would not pay his tithe when asked to. Yes, he would pay it in his own good time, but not when asked to. This makes for a hard living for a parson with a family to feed.

Many years later, when I was returning from Chelmsford on my bicycle after having watched an Essex cricket match, I saw the now elderly and bent frame of Mr Thurgood walking along the road. Even from a distance his pigeon-toed walk was quite unmistakable. I cycled up to him and got off my bicycle.

"Hello, sir," I said.

"W'hat?" came the reply.

"How are you, sir," I persevered.

"All right. And who the hell might you be?," he responded.

"Well sir, you may not remember me. But do you remember Mr Lucking," I asked.

His eyes scrutinised me for a moment and then his face lit up: "You are that little boy who used to come over with the dog, aren't you?"

"Yes, sir, that's me," I replied. "Those were wonderful days. I always enjoyed coming to your farm."

"Oh yes, I do remember you well," Mr Thurgood said. Then -- incredibly for those times -- he shook my hand.

We walked along the road, chatting about the old shooting days when I had come to his farm. As we approached the turning where our paths would normally have separated, I said to him:

"I am enjoying your company, sir. If it's all right with you, I'll walk along with you for a while." I was so very pleased at the delight in his face, and we continued reminiscing until we reached Diggin's drive.

"I say," he said to me. "Why don't you come over one

118

day. There is a barrel of cartridges in the house and plenty of guns. We could walk out together."

I never did, but I met Mr Thurgood again on many a friendly occasion thereafter.

By this time, Henry Lucking and most of Mr Thurgood's other sporting friends had given up shooting. As a result he invited one of his neighbours to shoot the land. Knowing quite how tricky Thurgood could be, the neighbour said, "But I don't know your land."

"Send your man over to old Jimmy Meyer at Little Laver. Ask him if you can have the services of his man. He knows my land as well as I do," Thurgood said.

Hence, the gamekeeper, who was a friend of mine, came to see Squire. His name was Winston Churchill. You might think this was a strange name for a local gamekeeper. It undoubtedly was. I can only assume that his parents had been great admirers of Winston Churchill during the Boer War.

"Would it be possible to borrow Fred Perry, sir?" Churchill asked. "We have an invitation to shoot Diggin's land on the condition that you'll let Fred come over and instruct me on the drives."

I was very chuffed by Thurgood's request and Squire readily agreed to let me go. Churchill and I set off on for Diggin's Farm to meet with Mr Thurgood.

"Come on in. Have some port," Mr Thurgood said, and took us into his sitting room. He poured three large glasses of port and we sat talking shooting stories for quite some time, the glasses regularly refilled. Churchill, fortunately, could drink port without any ill effect. I had discreetly used mine to water an aspidistra plant next to my chair.

"You'll do," Thurgood said composedly to Churchill. "You can hold your drink. Can't stand a man who can't hold his drink. Let's go and look at the drives."

And so, the shooting at Diggin's farm continued. Generally, Mr Thurgood did not join the shooting party. Only very occasionally did he condescend to shoot a pheasant, or rather, shoot at it. He lent the 1,000-acre farm to the Enville's syndicate and did not charge anything for the privilege. All he wanted in return was a brace or two of pheasants. He was quite content to let the guns get on with it, though he would keep an eye on them. Anybody who left a wounded bird behind or otherwise behaved in an unsportsmanlike fashion would be barred forever.

No matter how well I knew Diggin's farm by this time, Mr Thurgood baffled me one shooting day. "Fred, you take your dogs across and beat the tennis courts and then rejoin us over there," he briskly instructed me and then walked off.

Tennis courts? I had been at Diggin's God knows how often, but could not recall where the tennis courts were. I walked round the house and through the garden, but finally had to admit defeat. Oh dear, I thought, I have messed up. Mr Thurgood won't be very pleased that I have spoilt the drive. There was nothing for it but to go and join the other beaters. In order to get there, I and my dogs had to wrestle our way through a bed of nettles shoulder high and thistles as tall as a man.

"I don't know were I went wrong," I said to one of Thurgood's men. "I was supposed to have walked across the tennis courts."

"But you did," he replied. "That bed of nettles you have just come through, is the tennis courts."

One year, right at the end of the season, one of the guns shooting with the syndicate approached me:

"Perry, I have shot here several times now, but I have never seen Mr Thurgood. Most unusual. Come to think of it, I have seen very little activity on the farm. All I have seen since

I have been here was an old fellow spreading muck."

"But then you have seen him, sir," I replied earnestly, inwardly chuckling. "That was Mr Thurgood. He does not usually spread muck; he is just observing the shoot."

Mr Thurgood, somehow, contrived to be behind every drive -- just keeping an eye on things -- in working clothes, looking like a farm labourer.

Thurgood was indeed an extraordinary but very likeable man. One morning, he was walking down the lane towards Fyfield to get his newspapers. He was scruffily dressed as usual; smart clothes did not seem to feature in his priorities and he always looked more like a farm worker than the governor. An old tramp was standing by the roadside looking at the potato clamp. A potato clamp was a ridge or heap of potatoes at the edge of the field, thatched with straw to guard them against the elements.

"Is the governor about somewhere?" the tramp asked.

"No, I don't think so. Why?" Thurgood replied.

"I wanted to ask him if I could have a few of those potatoes," the tramp said, gesturing towards the clamp.

"Oh, that'll be all right. You go on then, get a few. And, I'll tell you one thing, the governor isn't a bad old sort. Go up to the farm at midday and ask if they'll give you a bit of bread."

"Would they?" The tramp's face lit up.

"Don't know," Thurgood mused, "but it's worth a try. As I said, he is not a bad chap."

When the tramp arrived at the house at lunchtime, Emily Johnston, the cook, opened the back door.

"They said that if I came here, you might perhaps give me a bit of bread," he mumbled meekly.

"Oh yes, do come into the kitchen. Sit yourself down," she said. "I have been told that you might be coming." And with that she placed a large, steaming plate of food in front of him.

When the tramp had finished this rare feast, he said: "I would very much like to thank the gentleman who owns this house. That was most kind of him." With that, the door opened on Thurgood: "You have your chance now. You had words with me this morning."

Thurgood was a real character. A shoot at his farm was always a wonderful occasion for me. Plenty of game. Once, I killed nine rabbits in one field without ever lifting a gun. Just knocked them over with my stick. They were so plentiful. But I always had to be jolly careful not to bring back too many rabbits, or Mr Lucking would have taken them from me.

Squire did not like going to Willingale any longer.

"Don't walk with those men," he would admonish. "I don't like the way they talk." He did not like the lusty stories and crude language used whenever Henry Lucking and Teddy Thurgood got together. I have never known either of them put a foot wrong with any of the servant girls, but they did like to tell coarse tales and would roar with laughter over them.

Thurgood died a few years later. True to character his last wish was: "When I die, just hook a set of horses off the harrow and take me for my last journey. No need to change your clothes."

And that is precisely what they did. They put him in an old tumble cart and in their scruffy old work clothes his men took him for burial at the village of Shellow Bowells. Why he wasn't buried at either of Willingale's two churches I am not quite sure, but my guess is that he had fallen out with both rectors again.

Chapter 10

The opening meet of the Essex Hunt always took place on Matching Green -- a splendid spectacle which to this day I thoroughly enjoy. It was always a very special occasion for the village and had the festive atmosphere of a fete. All the villagers

Hunt Meet on Matching Green - 1885
Leaves from a Hunting Diary in Essex, by H Beauchamp Yerburgh, 1900

were out on the Green watching the first meet of the season and somehow it seemed that all errands took servants from miles around via the Green on that day. Many farmers and their families arrived by pony trap from the surrounding areas.

The schoolmaster would close the school for an hour or two in the morning while the hunt was assembling. Providing we children kept at a respectable distance, we were allowed to be on the Green and watch the colourful goings-on as the gentry, estate owners and wealthy farmers met for the start of another hunting season. During the season commencing on that day, hunting was to keep them very busy. The hunt usually met four days a week. Estates and farms were left in the, hopefully, capable hands of their managers.

The Countess of Warwick usually arrived in a carriage drawn by four horses. She would alight -- there is no other word for it -- from her carriage and be helped on to her horse by her groom. She always looked extremely beautiful and regal to me as she sat side-saddle on her horse, dressed in a smart black riding habit with a tailored jacket over an immaculately buttoned down white waistcoat and a crisp white stock. Her beautiful blond hair was fashioned into a bun on which a black silk top hat sat jauntily and her skirt was so gracefully draped over the horse's flank as if it had been arranged fold by fold for a painting, showing just a little of the shining black leather boots. I am told that underneath the specially tailored hunting skirts the lady riders wore breeches.

Countess of Warwick
The Essex Foxhounds, by R F Gilbey
& T Gilbey, 1896

Sometimes she would even wear a scarlet coat -- the colour normally referred to as 'hunting pink'. She was the only one of the lady riders daring enough to wear hunting pink rather than the traditional black jackets for women. Friends in the hunting fraternity have since told me that there were two other women who were daring enough to wear the pink -- or powerful enough to get away with it: the Empress of Austria and the Countess of Feversham. Anybody else would have been sent home by the master of the hunt for wearing inappropriate dress.

We were fascinated by the glamour of the Countess of Warwick, especially as gossip had it that she had been the mistress of King Edward VII and that he had a railway station built at her estate 'Easton Lodge' for his private use.

In later years, she arrived at Matching Green in a Rolls Royce car rather than her carriage and I have always felt that she lost some of her regal air to the process of motorization.

Countess of Warwick
Leaves from a Hunting Diary in Essex,
by H Beauchamp Yerburgh, 1900

The opening meet was much loved by children and adults alike. It provided a glimpse into the wonderful and glamorous world of fox hunting.

Assisted by their grooms, the huntsmen would mount their splendidly groomed horses and then parade across the Green, stopping to have a chat with a fellow rider and occasionally throwing a few coppers down to us children. We would scrabble to find them, with the lucky ones being able to buy a few biscuits or sweets later. The hounds would rush around, eagerly yapping in anticipation of the fun ahead.

Servants from one of the bigger houses on the Green would then arrive with trays carrying the stirrup cups for the huntsmen.

At eleven o'clock the horn sounded and the hunt moved off the Green down the lane towards one of the woods followed for a while by a whole posse of onlookers and followers. Henry Lucking, like most farmers, was a keen follower of the hunt and would invariably have taken the day off to watch the hunt and the local farmers were in most instances quite understanding if the labourers wanted to take a few hours off for the occasion as long as they made up the lost time on another day.

We children unfortunately had to go back to school once the hunt had left the Green. But on rare occasions the school would stay closed for the day. We knew exactly where to wait, depending upon which covert was the first to be drawn. The challenge was to anticipate which way the pack of hounds was heading and to be there ready to open the gates for the hunt. Every single field or meadow had a gate as livestock would be kept there at some time or other during the year. Hence, we were often able to save the hunt some tricky jumps or a lot of time dismounting to open and close the gates. This ensured a few pennies for us children. Another good earner was to observe if any riders had lost their hats in the runs, as a swift return of the missing attire would be rewarded by a tip.

For several seasons running, whenever the hunt drew Brick Kiln Wood I knew what was going to happen next. The fox invariably came across the fields behind Waterman's End. In particular, I remember one lovely dark-coated fox. His fur shone like polished bronze and his brush swept the ground. I saw him stop, scratch his ear like a dog, then he looked over his shoulder like a regular cool customer to see where the hounds were and ambled off again. He never looked is if he felt particularly threatened. The hounds fanned out across the heavy, ploughed field, followed by a straggling line of sportsmen. Charlie waited for them to close in, trotted past Waterman's End, across the field and shortly thereafter we would hear the horn sound the signal 'gone away'. The hounds always lost the fox in the same position. It took us a long time to work out what had happened to the fox on each of those occasions. The hunt was obliged to leave this fox to live for another day. Cunning Charlie had outsmarted them and had gone to ground in the burial vault at High Laver church yard.

Over the years, my relationship with old Charlie Fox has always been an uneasy one. He is extremely beautiful; he is undoubtedly the most clever and crafty animal I know of and, equally, he is undoubtedly the greatest menace to poultry and game birds alike. I have admired him and have taken my children into the woods at night to enjoy the lovely sight of the vixen playing with her cubs. I have shot some to protect my employer's poultry, but often I enjoyed seeing him amble away and I have never ceased to marvel at his cunning.

I once saw the hunt in pursuit of a fox which looked exhausted. I was working in the fields when I heard the sounds of the hunt approaching. And sure enough a panting, tired-looking fox trotted past me and disappeared into the top of a hollow willow tree just down the road from Waterman's End. The hounds had lost sight but were still following the scent. As they got within a few hundred yards of the willow, another bigger fox emerged out of the bottom of the hollow tree and he was away like a shot. The hounds followed but eventually lost him. The first, tired fox remained safely hidden in the tree until the hunt had long departed. Is it not astonishing to think that the fox is smart enough to run a relay race with his peers and outsmart a pack of hounds and the huntsmen. Truly he is an artful dodger.

I recall another amusing incident which took place while the hunt was on our land. Mr Lucking and I had been out shooting rabbits. As we shot them, we would hang the rabbits neatly on the hedge. Our attention was drawn to the hunt approaching and as we turned and followed the fox's progress we heard the hounds yapping behinds us, expecting them to come rushing past at any moment. The fox was definitely getting away and as we turned round to see what had happened to the hounds, we found that they had snatched most of our rabbits off the hedge and were munching away at what had been intended to be the Luckings' supper.

During the season the hunt would meet several times on Matching Green and at surrounding farms, but to me the occasion was never quite as special as the first one, the opening meet.

The annual hunt ball of the Essex Hunt was held at Down Hall, the biggest local manor house. The following morning, the hunt would usually meet again on Matching Green.

Down Hall lies about two miles from Matching Green and was by far the biggest employer in our area. It kept about forty house staff and seven gardeners. Local people considered themselves very fortunate to be employed at Down Hall. The pay would be a little better and one could catch a glimpse of the glamorous life their occupants led.

At the beginning of the century, Down Hall had been

owned by Lord Rookwood, previously Sir Henry Selwin-Ibbetson, who had been our local member of parliament from 1868 to 1892. He had been immensely popular locally and by all accounts had been a good parliamentarian.

Lord Rookwood
The Essex Foxhounds,
by R F Gilbey & T Gilbey, 1896

When he resigned his seat and was elevated to the peerage, he took the name of one of his farms, Rookwood Hall, which neighboured my Squire's estate.

Lady Rookwood
Leaves from a Hunting Diary in Essex,
by H Beauchamp Yerburgh, 1900

Lord Rookwood had married three times, but died without issue in 1902.

The villagers always chuckled indulgently: "He wasn't smart enough to let the butler or a footman have a try."

His heir was Major Horace Calverley. We did not see much of Major Calverley, but the handsome, Honourable Mrs Calverley was much in residence. As was her friend, a Major Tufnel.

Mrs Calverley was a striking figure at the hunt. But for all her good looks, my Squire was not impressed. Whilst he thoroughly approved of anybody participating in the hunt, he always referred to her as a 'brazen hussy'. In latter years I was fortunate enough to participate in some of the Down Hall servants' balls and I can only vouch for the fact that she was indeed a very good-looking woman.

On the evening of one particular hunt ball, when I was still a boy, I was very keen to get away from work at Waterman's End as early as possible. I wanted to get back to the Green. There was always the possibility that I might catch a glimpse of a carriage driving the guests, in all their glorious finery, to the ball.

But Mr Lucking had spotted me before I could get away. "Freddie John, tell Albert Clarke (the stockman), that I want to go ferreting tomorrow," he ordered. "I want you two to meet me at Little Laver Lodge at nine o'clock sharp."

When I told Albert Clarke he grumbled a little, but I knew that he really loved ferreting, and he agreed soon enough. I ran back to the Green as quickly as possible and met my friends. Together we hid behind a hedge and watched the goings-on at Down Hall as carriage after carriage arrived, interspersed with the occasional car -- even a couple of Rolls Royces.

Next morning I walked to Little Laver Lodge for the nine o'clock meeting. I was, as usual, the ferret boy. I took the ferret out of its box and popped it into the rabbit hole. Mr Lucking was standing, his gun cocked, prepared to shoot any rabbit that might be chased out. Albert Clark was there ready to dig the ferrets out in case they got 'laid up', meaning that they stayed down the hole trying to get the rabbit for their own consumption.

"Morning," Basil Gingell, the farmer from High Laver Grange, shouted. Having spotted Henry Lucking from the road, he had pulled up in his car to have a word with his neighbour. Suddenly, right behind him the chauffeur-driven Rolls Royce carrying Mr Tyser appeared. He was a local hunt big-wig and on his way to the traditional post-hunt ball meet at Down Hall.

Wham! Crash! The Rolls Royce drove straight into the back Mr Gingell's small Ford car, virtually mounting it.

Mr Tyser, all spruced up in his hunting pink, climbed out of his car. Purple with fury he pointed his finger at Basil Gingell and shouted: "God damn it, man, look what you have done to my car. You incompetent fool! I'll see you in court for that."

Turning to Mr Lucking, he spluttered: "What do you think of that."

"Whatever I have to say, I'll say in court," replied Mr Lucking, most courteously.

Eventually the case was taken to the County Court at Chelmsford: Tyser v Gingell.

Mr Lucking was called to the hearing as a witness and questioned by counsel: "With whom, Mr Lucking, does the blame lie in this case?"

"Well, the gentleman in the Rolls Royce, of course. The Rolls Royce misbehaved," he replied.

"What exactly do you mean, Mr Lucking?" counsel asked.

"Exactly what I said. The Rolls Royce misbehaved," Mr Lucking said stubbornly.

"Please, sir, I must insist upon clarification. What exactly do you mean when you say the Rolls Royce misbehaved? And, I put it to you that at the time of the accident, you were catching your ferret and not in a position to observe what happened," counsel said impatiently.

Mr Lucking's chest bulged as he replied unflinchingly: "And I put it to you that I have my man to catch my ferret. And -- the Rolls Royce was misbehaving."

At this point the press corps in the gallery started giggling. Obviously somebody was getting the better of this snooty barrister.

Mr Lucking then addressed the bench: "I'll tell you my

lord, the Rolls Royce was indeed misbehaving. I said so to my man: 'We see something new every day. But I have never before seen a Ford motor car f****d by a Rolls Royce'."

The judge found in favour of Gingell, and Mr Tyser had to pay all the costs. As the parties were walking out of the courtroom, Tyser turned to Henry Lucking and said: "There are liars, there are damn liars, and there are bloody liars!"

"See you next year then," Mr Lucking calmly replied. "We'll be there ferreting -- and mind you keep your eye on the road."

And that was how it became a tradition to go ferreting at Little Laver Lodge the morning after the hunt ball. Once or twice during the ensuing years we saw Mr Tyser drive past on his way to the hunt meet -- accompanied by our laughter.

Chapter 11

In the winter, when we were unable to work in the fields, either because the land was resting or because the ground was frozen, all sorts of other tasks would be undertaken by the farm labourers. There were always buildings to be repaired and tackle to be mended.

As soon as the shooting season was over, invariably one of the local farmers or estate managers would call round and ask for the loan of labourers for wood clearing. This suited our employers well as they did not have to meet our wage bill during that period in the winter. We would be temporarily transferred to the employment of the other farmer and he would pay us during the duration.

"You can have the bloody lot," would be Henry Lucking's inevitable reply to such a request.

Then he would turn to us and grin: "None of you are any good."

Often the men, as well as the horses and their keepers from all the surrounding farms, would be hired out for weeks at a time. There were many woods in our neighbourhood: Brick Kiln Wood, Man Wood, Bury Wood, Priory Wood, Colville Hall Wood, Down Hall Wood and Matching Park. They covered hundreds of acres. I regret to say that many of them were lost to American airfields in the Second World War.

Wood management was quite an art. It was just as important to the farmer as dealing with his arable land. He would rely heavily on the income from the timber. To keep a wood in good order, it would have to be coppiced regularly, with the old timber taken out to give the new growth a chance. Or, mature timber would have to be felled and replanted with new tree stock.

Major tree felling was always undertaken by a specialist team who arrived with their 'Timberwhim', a low carriage wagon to cart the large tree trunks away. It was wonderful to see how artfully horses with chains and pulleys would drag the timber out of the wood.

"Polly pull! Tiger pull!" the horsekeeper would softly call to the horses. The horses were harnessed to a steering shaft with Polly as the tracer horse in front and Tiger behind. Each one knew exactly what to do. The old horsekeepers were totally in tune with their animals. I am sure they virtually lived with them and had often brought them up from foals.

On the farmer's instructions we would deal with small trees, bushes and hedges and generally clear up the almighty mess created by tree felling. Then the trunks might be cut into suitable lengths and loaded onto the strongest carts available. These carts took a lot of punishment from the weight of the timber. Their great big iron wheels created deep ruts.

Then they would set off to deliver the timber to places like the local breweries. Breweries had a great appetite for wood to keep their copper heated. Smaller trees and branches would be cut up into fencing poles. All fences were made of wood. Barbed wire was banned in those days for the sake of livestock and horses.

Some of the wood would be kept for use on the estate or farm, but most would be sold like a crop.

Every scrap of wood was gathered up for use, right down to making bundles of faggots for use on the fire. Making neat, tight bundles of faggots was another a skilful task. First the ties needed to hold the faggots together had to be made. This was done by cutting a long sliver of elm wood and twisting it round and round until you were left with a pliable, wooden cord. This would be laid on the ground and faggot wood stacked tightly on top until the bundle was roughly the size of the average sheaf of wheat. Now it had to be tightly tied together so that it could not accidentally fall apart again while being handled.

Ditches would be cleared and gullies cut to let the water run off. The woods would then be left nice and tidy with plenty of space for the new growth to develop.

We always kept twelve to fourteen working horses at the farm. Mr Lucking preferred Suffolk Punches to any other breed. They were strong horses and had beautifully clean legs. Shire horses with hairy -- or 'feathered' -- legs, had proved difficult for our farm work. Huge clumps of mud would have attached themselves to a shire's legs, necessitating regular stops to wash them down. This, as you can imagine, is not an easy undertaking in the middle of a field when the nearest water pump might be half a mile away.

Hence, Henry Lucking had changed to the very popular Suffolks some years earlier. He would travel great distances, to horse sales in Bury St Edmunds, for instance, to buy good stock. He was an excellent horse farmer and he loved his horses.

We had three horsekeepers at the farm. Each horsekeeper looked after, and worked with, three or four horses. Henry Lucking would breed his own horses too. Therefore the horsekeepers also had to look after pregnant mares and the young colts being brought on.

Their work started at five in the morning and the first task would be to comb and brush the horses. This would clear them of insects and stop their coats from matting. The grooming would finish with the horse getting its tail and/or mane plaited into a neat braid and tied with a horse ribbon. The horses would feed while being groomed.

In summer the horses very often would be waiting for you at the meadow gate or you would call them, and snorting loudly, they would gallop over to you.

In the winter, however, they were housed in stables. Depending on what work was planned for the day, the horse would be fitted with a chain harness for working on the land or a cart harness if it would be pulling a cart.

Then the horsekeeper would open the stable door and the animals would walk out into the yard in readiness for the day's work.

Early in the farming season, the first task was to get the land ready by giving it a top dressing of fertiliser. Horses would be hitched to the cart, and the day labourers, having arrived for their starting time of seven o'clock, would load the fertiliser bags onto the cart. Mind, mostly these bags weighed a hundred-weight, but some weighed two hundred-weight -- in other words 224 pounds. The farmer would have instructed one of his trusted men as to how much fertiliser per acre he wanted on the field.

The driver of the horse cart would drop the bags of fertiliser at appropriate intervals along the headlands. Then the workers would fill what were called skips, which were actually cloth bags, with fertiliser. The bag would be hung over the shoulders at a comfortable height enabling the bearer to reach inside, scoop the powder up by hand and distribute it over the ground. The skill was to throw it up and let the wind distribute it. Only experienced men would be trusted to get the quantities right.

The next job of the season was to harrow the expensive fertiliser in. This, depending on the size of the harrow, would need two or three horses. The horses' chains would be attached to the 'whippletree', and this in turn attached to the harrow. A whippletree was a piece of wood which dragged horizontally behind the horses and kept the harrow flat on the ground.

The horsekeeper would call the lead horse's name, "Captain", jerk the plough lines and both horses would set off side by side.

"Come on, Captain. Come. Get over," he would instruct the horse, gently tugging the lines to keep the harrow in a straight line. The horses knew exactly how to respond.

All day long the horsekeeper and the horses would walk up and down the field until the field was completely harrowed.

The head horsekeeper would now follow on with a drill to sow the seed corn. This was only done by the trusted, most senior and experienced man as the entire crop would depend on the job being done properly.

The drill was like a long trough containing the seed corn, with seed culters, or spouts, coming out of the bottom, spaced differently depending on the crop. The drill had a large wheel on each end which would leave a nice clear wheel track as it went along. The entire drill was connected with three pieces of wood forming a triangle to the steering bar. The horsekeeper would walk along and, using the steerage, keep the horses straight.

Fred Perry working with a horse

Another man walked behind the drill. His job also was very critical. He would walk back and forth along the drill keeping a careful eye on the corn making sure it dropped through the spouts. A blockage would have resulted in a bare patch.

If a seed spout did get blocked, as happened frequently, you would stop the horses and seed by hand. Before setting off again you had to throw a little seed in front of the drill to avoid another bare patch when the horses got going again.

Coming to the end of the field, the farm hand would

pull the lever which blocked the seed spouts. The horses and drill would be turned to face the opposite direction and the wheel would be aligned to run along the track created by sowing the first row. This method ensured lovely straight drills with quite even sowing.

"Do you need any more corn?" I recall a horseman asking the farm hand in charge of the drill after they had been sowing for some time. "You must be nearly out"

"Oh no, still got plenty of corn," came the reply.

After a while, the horsekeeper asked again and got the same reply. His experience told the horsekeeper that by now they should have been out of corn and he stopped the horses to have a look himself.

"You bloody fool," swore the horsekeeper. "You haven't bloody well put the lever down. Wait till the governor hears of this. You'll be sacked. And you deserve to be!" he added furiously.

They had indeed spent the best part of the morning going over the field without sowing a single grain. Not only that, the drill wheels had left its deep tracks and now there was nothing for it but to send the harrow in again and start all over again.

Following the drilling team would be another horsekeeper with a light harrow attached to one horse gently raking in the seeds.

A special aptitude for drilling was needed and a great deal of patience and diligence. I became quite good at it and enjoyed it. I took such pride in my work that I would often get on my bicycle in my own spare time and visit the field after a few weeks to see how the seed had set. Hopefully I would find neat rows of sprouting crop without bare patches.

Much of the success of the crop, from now on, depended on the weather. To give the crop as good a chance as possible, however, the weeds had to be kept at bay by hoeing. When growing a cereal crop, local women would be employed to clear the weeds. Docks and thistles were our worst enemy. The women used a two-pronged fork, called a docking iron, to dig the docks out and a sharp-edged blade to cut the thistles down. Then they would carry the weeds off the field. For this labour they received one shilling a day. Other crops like turnip or mangolds, used as cattle feed, would be hoed by a horse plough first and then manually hoed in between the plants.

Mr Lucking on the whole stayed clear of potatoes as they were very labour intensive. They had to be set, weeded and picked all by hand.

About a month before harvesting, we would cut the grass verges back. All the birds nesting there would have hatched their young by then. The farmer would watch the ripening of the crop very carefully.

"If the corn looks ripe," Mr Lucking would say, "give it another week." When the time was right, four men would go into the field with their scythes, just inside the gate, and cut an area clear just big enough for the binder and the horses to fit in. This corn would be tied by hand, but thereafter the binder would take over. The binder would cut and tie the corn, and then throw the sheaves out along its path. A gang of eight men would follow the binder, pick up the sheaves and in tandem stand them up into a double row of four sheaves making a stook, or trave. The sheaves would not just be stood up but also pressed hard into the stubble. This anchored them quite firmly to the ground, so that even a fairly strong wind would not blow them over.

"The corn should hear the church bells ring on three Sundays," was the expression the farmers used, meaning that by this time all green stuff would have died down in the stooks and the corn would be ready for stacking. To make certain, they would rub an ear of corn, throw it in the air and if it separated it was ready.

We took great pride in making our stacks. We would have to look at them -- and hear Mr Lucking's swearing about an untidy stack -- until the following spring. And the stacks would have to withstand the winter wind and weather.

First we would make the stack bottom. This was made of layers of hedge or brushwood which we had laid out in readiness during the winter clearing. In the absence of sufficient wood we would have to use straw, but this was not as satisfactory as it did not provide such good ventilation. The bottom would be stacked about three feet tall and now the making of the cornstack would begin.

Day labourers, thus named because they were hired only on a daily basis and could be let go in the evening -- there was little job security then -- would bring the corn stooks off the field and place the cart right next to the stack bottom.

We preferred making round cornstacks, which were a little more difficult to get shaped well, but with the advantage that they had no corners for the wind to catch and loosen. The first step was to create a round stook in the centre, thereafter to lay sheaves up to the level of the string of the previous sheaf until the edge was reached. The next layer would be placed in the gaps of the previous layer of sheaves. In this way corn was tightly packed and the centre always remained higher than the outer rim. Labourers would stand on the cart and fetch the corn up with a pitchfork, while the actual stacking was carried out by the binder and the stacker.

When the cornstack became too big to reach -- remember that cornstacks were taller than houses -- the elevator was brought out. The best way I can describe an elevator is to compare it with an escalator as we know it today. It was chain-driven, and the sheaves were put on spikes and transported up. The whole contraption was driven by a little pony walking a treadmill.

In later years it was driven by a small diesel engine which certainly saved the little pony a lot of hard labour. Sometimes we would even send a cup of tea up on the elevator in the hope that the man at the top was nimble enough to grab it before it went over.

Once the cornstack was completed, the next task was to thatch it. My grandfather had been a thatcher and I guess it may have been in the blood. My Uncle Jimmy had been good and like him I became quite competent at thatching.

On the other hand, my great grandfather had been a sawyer yet I never showed any inclination for life in the sawpit. What a hard job -- one man standing over the saw pit and one in it -- the long saw blade being pulled between them, sawing up huge trunks of wood. This was the only way tree trunks could be sawn into planks before the day of electric saws. I have been told that the men in the bottom of the pit often went blind because so much sawdust had fallen into their eyes.

Somebody might have thought of inventing a pair of goggles to protect their eyes, but in those days workers just accepted their 'lot' as a fact of life. Labour was cheap and, after all, most inventions were designed to make the life of the ruling classes more comfortable and only filtered down to the working classes much later. Goggles were most probably invented for early motorists or pilots in open planes.

Thatching was much more to my liking. At first I had to shake up a huge heap of straw and wet it down with pails of water. Once it was thoroughly damp, it became much more pliable and when pulled, a bundle of it would come out nice

141

and straight. This bundle was called a yellam. Five yellams would be laid at slight angles onto a piece of string on the ground and tied up. To have a good yellam maker was a tremendous help.

When the yellams were sent up to the top of the haystack the thatcher could untie the bundle and lay the yellams almost as easily as tiles. The first yellams were laid at the edge of the stack, tucked in, then tied and pegged down, making sure the pegs went in at an angle or the rain would run down them into the stack. Then the thatcher worked gently up the roof to the pinnacle. There he would insert a stout stick and tie it very securely and tightly. I would often tie a little flag or an old handkerchief in with it, just for fun.

One year I recall thatching sixteen stacks at Waterman's End and Little Laver Grange.

Chapter 12

"Well, men," Henry Lucking said. "It's time to call the relieving officer in. I am getting a bit short of money."

The relieving officer was Mr Lucking's term for the threshing machine. He wanted some corn threshed so that he could sell it and bring in some cash. In other instances, he might have wanted to sell because the market conditions were particularly favourable.

"I'll talk to the other farmers," he would say. "We might be able to get the machine booked a bit sooner if the contractor has plenty of work in our area."

I was standing next to Squire in the farmyard, when in strode Henry Lucking, visibly in a bad temper.

"The machine is coming the day after tomorrow and somebody is having my coal," he said to Squire. "Everyday some more disappears. Who could it be? I'll catch them."

Coal had been piled up near the corn stacks as it would be needed for operating the threshing machine.

"Have you got a bottle of whisky?" Mr Lucking asked Squire. "I'll make it right with you afterwards."

"What do you want a bottle of whisky for, Henry?"

"I am not going to sit there all night perished by cold without a drop of whisky," Mr Lucking explained, "and I plan to sit there all night to catch the bugger."

Squire turned to me: "Fred, pop to the cellar and see if there is a bottle of whisky."

I went to the cellar and took a bottle of Squire's whisky and carried it back to Mr Lucking. He tucked the bottle in his jacket pocket, where it all but disappeared. Henry Lucking was such a large man, that even his pockets seemed oversized. His plan was to sit by the cornstacks, well concealed by straw.

"How did you get on, Henry?" Squire asked the next morning. "Who did it?" We were all anxiously hanging around the yard to hear whom Mr Lucking had caught.

But Mr Lucking wasn't looking very cheerful. He took off his sugar pudding hat and scratched his bald head.

"Well," he said, "I waited and then I had a sip of whisky. Nobody came, and I had another sip of whisky. It got quite cold, and I had another sip. I drank a lot of that bloody whisky. And when I woke up, the rest of the coal was gone."

Even Squire could not contain a chuckle as he walked back to the house.

A new supply of coal was laid on and the threshing machine arrived on the appointed day. It looked really more like a huge caravan than a machine. It was twenty to twenty-five yards long, pulled by a huge steam engine. The racket it made could be heard miles away.

The din of the threshing machine was only ever surpassed by the huge steam ploughs. Whenever they had to pass through a village or small town, the local bobby would walk some way ahead and warn all occupants of the impending passing of the huge monster.

The enormous engine created so much vibration, that all ornaments, glass jars and such items had to be removed from window sills, mantelpieces, shelves or shop windows. Everything shook and rattled as it passed and the noise was absolutely deafening.

Only once in my working life have I known Lucking to call in the steam plough when, one year, we were rather behind with the ploughing.

But the arrival of the threshing machine was a regular feature of our farming life.

It invariably arrived with a gang of nine or ten very rough men. The job of thresher was the lowest of the low on the farm workers' totem pole. It was the hottest, dirtiest, dustiest job imaginable, with plenty of rats and mice thrown in for company.

Yet, as a small boy I had not known that, and it had been my sincerest wish to become a thresher. The reason was simple, they would always buy themselves chunks of bacon and fry it on the huge coal shovel over the red hot engine. The smell had been so inviting to a grumbling belly, that I had been sure that this was the work for me. As I grew up, I soon changed my mind.

Even having to hump the heavy sacks of corn from the threshing machine on to your shoulders, on to the cart and later into the barn was better than being a thresher. Talking about heavy sacks, a sack of oats weighed twelve stone, whilst barley, wheat, beans and clover weighed fourteen, sixteen, eighteen and twenty stone respectively [twenty stone = 280 English pounds].

The threshing machine might turn out 120 to 130 sacks of corn in a day. And it always surprised me how many of the labourers developed weak bladders, bad backs, bad feet, or any other ailment which had not troubled them before as soon as it was time to shift the corn sacks.

At the end of the day, when every single sack had been stacked into our best barn, the dressing barn, I would be utterly exhausted.

How my old friend, Peter Peacock, managed this heavy work all these years I shall never understand. Peter was always a slight man and weighed just over nine stone.

Yet Peter spent his entire life at Matching Hall carting heavy weights. He must have carried hundreds of tons of potatoes alone -- often over a plank covering the ditch from the field to vehicle.

Matching Hall & Church
Leaves from a Hunting Diary in Essex, by H Beauchamp Yerburgh, 1900

The hardest was lifting the one hundred-weight sacks off the ground and throwing them over your shoulder. That was the most back-breaking part.

Common sense dictates that Peter's muscles and joints should be worn out, but there he is in his 100th year and a well man. The only 'break' Peter ever had was when he joined the Royal Artillery during the First World War. There he had the 'lighter' task of loading the ammunition. If you listen to him today, he considers that period the only recreational break in his life.

I have always hated threshing and didn't mind one bit when combine harvesters became available. But that was many, many years later. Long before then, another God-send was invented -- the sack lifter. This was a chain-driven cranker that lifted the sacks to shoulder heights. That was a great help and saved our backs a lot of strain.

"Bloody rats!" Henry Lucking shouted as he stormed into the farmyard some days later. "They're in the dressing barn. They are gnawing the sacks to pieces. If we don't do something about it, we will not have any grain left."

"Have you seen them, Freddie John?" he roared.

"No sir, I haven't. The dressing barn is locked up. Only the stockman is allowed to go in there," I replied.

"Well, you are allowed to go in there now. Here are the keys," he said, slamming a bunch of keys on the table.

"You'll take care of the rats, Freddie John." Then he hesitated for a moment. "I'll give you a penny for each rat caught. Yes! A penny a tail."

I crossed the farmyard into the garden of Little Laver Grange to see Squire. "Where have you been, Fred?" he asked.

"I have been with Mr Lucking. He wants me to take care of the rats in the dressing barn. He says that they are eating everything in sight. May I please borrow the rat-traps, sir?"

"Typical," Squire shrugged. "Mr Lucking should have taken care of this much earlier. Yes. Yes, you may take the rat-traps."

I found forty rat traps in various stages of rusty disrepair and took them over to the barn. With odd bits of wire I rendered as many as possible functional and set them all over the dressing barn, carefully concealed under half drain pipes and whatever else I could find around. I carefully re-locked the barn, took my bicycle and went home.

All during supper, I kept thinking: I wonder how many rats I have caught? How many pennies will I get? My curiosity got the better of me, and late in the evening I cycled back to check my rat traps.

Hurrah! Nearly every one had a rat in it. I was immensely pleased with myself. I took the dead rats out of the traps and reset them all again. Next morning, I arrived especially early and found that, again, nearly all the traps had sprung.

"Here mate," Albert Clarke, the old stockman said, "we'll lay a bit of tilt over them. The governor will be 'ere presently."

And with that, Henry Lucking came riding into the yard, his bicycle frame creaking under his huge weight.

"How did you get on with the rats?" he shouted. "I want to see the tails, Freddie John."

"Oh, you can see more than tails," said the old stockman and, with a flourish yanked the bit of cloth off the almost eighty dead rats.

Henry Lucking looked at my bounty, took his time of lighting his pipe, and slowly walked around the rats.

"I'm not going to give you a penny each for that lot. Half of these buggers would have died of old age. I am only going to pay you for the young ones."

By golly, Mr Lucking was tight-fisted. Despite his trying to deprive a little farm lad of a few pennies because the rats were of pensionable age, I still really liked him. Mind you, I had to laugh -- even then. You have to have a sense of humour. If you can see the funny side, nothing seems half as bad. When I took the rat-traps back to the house, Squire made up my shortfall -- as he did on many other occasions.

Chapter 13

Squire was a most kind and generous man. He was always ready to help out whenever he could. When I was a boy, he always made it possible for me to earn a little extra. He would send me on errands after my working day. Often he would ask me to cycle to Ongar to fetch something.

"Fred. Do you feel like cycling to Ongar for me this evening?" he would ask. "I quite fancy a nice piece of fresh fish for this evening. Mr Kent, the fishmonger, has the best fish in the area."

After I returned with the fish and delivered it to the kitchen, I went to see Squire to give him his change.

" No, you keep those. I don't want any fishy smelling coppers in my pocket, what!" he would say, waving away my hand with the change.

When I was a little older, he would regularly send me to the post office with a cheque:

"Bring me back five pounds in half crowns," he would say.

"Can't give less than a half crown, what!" he would add, talking more to himself than me.

He always kept a handful of half crowns in his trouser pocket and handed them out to any poor labourer we might meet on our walks around the estate.

"Have you seen any birds?" he would ask the passing man.

"Yes sir, I saw a nice one as I passed along the wood," the labourer would reply.

As regular as clockwork, Squire would then delve into his pocket and extract a coin:

"Catch!" he would exclaim. "Here's half a crown."

Yet even Squire sometimes could not grasp just how poor people really were, and how his class was able to make people tremble in their boots as he and his likes held the absolute power.

Over the years, as Squire came to trust me more, he often asked my advice on occasions. Sometimes I even felt confident enough to offer an opinion without being asked. As on the occasion when we found a brightly painted gypsy caravan parked along the wide verge down Watery Lane. A young, well-turned out, gypsy man was tethering the horse to a gatepost and his young wife was crouching in the caravan cradling a baby.

"What do you think you are doing here? Do you not realize that you are trespassing," Squire instantly challenged the gypsy.

"Would it be possible for me to stay for a little while, sir? the gypsy enquired. "My wife is not very well."

"Don't argue with me or I'll get the police here," Squire commanded. "Leave my land immediately." With that Squire angrily stomped off down the lane, followed reluctantly by myself.

"That was a bit harsh, sir," I ventured an uninvited comment after a while.

Squire just walked on as if he had not heard me. He strode on for several hundred yards further, angrily swinging his shooting stick. Then he suddenly halted, stuck his shooting stick into the ground and turned around to face me:

"What do you mean, Fred?" he demanded huffily. "Do you think I was too harsh?"

"Well, sir," I replied. "They weren't doing any harm. He did seem like quite a nice and polite fellow and his wife is clearly quite ill. You might have let them stay a few days."

"The gypsy is most probably harnessing his horse now, feeling quite desperate and his wife will be crying her eyes out," I added.

150

Before I had even quite finished the sentence he had already taken a few brisk steps back in direction of the gypsies. His waxed moustache quivered at the thought of having caused such misery.

When we reached the site of the caravan again, the gypsy was indeed in the process of breaking camp and looked rather worried as he saw Squire briskly walking up to him.

"Forget all I said," Squire said, taking a piece of paper out of his pocket. "I was rather harsh." Then he leaned on a gate post and wrote a note.

"Here," he said, passing the note to the gypsy. "You might need a doctor for your wife? Take this to the post office and they will get one for you."

Then, as I have seen him do so often, he took out his wallet and gave the man ten bob.

"You can stay as long as you like," he added. "And here is another note. This one is for police in case they try to move you on. You have my permission to stay on my land." In conclusion, he then instructed me to give them the two rabbits we had shot earlier, before strutting off again.

Thereafter Squire would ask me each day if I had been past the gypsies. "Are they all right?" he would want to know. This gypsy family was indeed a very decent one and made their living by picking crops. They had come to Essex for the pea picking and would eventually finish up in Kent for the hop harvest. By the time they moved on a couple of weeks later, the wife and child were much healthier and happier looking than when we had first set eyes on them.

Squire took great delight in having been able to help, but not once on these occasions did he acknowledge that it had been my speaking out that had caused him to change his mind.

I can recall a similar incident when he nearly turned one of the cottagers out for setting a snare. The poor man was only trying to protect his crop from the rabbits, but unfortunately the Squire's dog, Punch, had got caught in the snare. On this occasion too, he reversed his instructions and they were not evicted.

Squire was a pillar of society, as straight and honest as I have ever known any man. He was well-respected as a magistrate for being fair and conscientious. Yet he would only adjudicate if the case fell within the bounds of his experience and if there was no possible conflict of interest.

For example, he would not sit on motoring cases. "I cannot possibly adjudicate on this as I am not a motorist myself," he would say.

Nor would he take his place on the bench if the case was a paternity suite or a bastardy case. "Gentlemen, if I might be excused," he would say. "I don't really understand the details as I am not a parent."

I recall another case when he would not hear a particular case because the incident had taken place on his land. One Saturday morning, one of the horsekeepers came to the house.

"There is a gang of caravans parked near the gravel pit," he reported. "I saw the gypsies walking across the field with some greyhounds. They mean mischief, sir."

"Fred," Squire turned to me, "go to Moreton and talk to the constable. Tell him that I suggest that he get backup from Ongar."

When I delivered the message to the constable, he sneered at the idea of help. "I do not need any assistance," he said grandly. "I'll soon sort them out. I know how to deal with these people."

With that we got on to our bicycles and rode back to

Little Laver. I offered to come along with him to help deal with the ruffians, but he turned me down.

When I told Squire, he just shrugged his shoulders, but it was barely two hours before the horsekeeper was back.

"I found the policeman crawling along the road bleeding from his head," he informed Squire. He had apparently taken the injured policeman to the nearest house where the blood had been washed off and a bandage applied.

The gypsies had viciously attacked the policeman with a big spanner and it was only his police helmet which saved him from more extensive injuries. The helmet was totally smashed, but the badge had remained intact.

Now it was definitely time for assistance. Despite his head wound, the constable insisted on going along with his colleagues for the chase.

Meanwhile, of course, the gypsies had hitched their horses and made a hasty escape. The police commandeered two local cars and caught up with the gypsies a few miles down the road. All were arrested and charged with assaulting a police officer.

Squire could not adjudicate and the case was heard by somebody else. He told me later how disgusted he had been at the leniency of the verdict, a five pound fine. One of the old gypsy women had just lifted her filthy voluminous skirts and extracted a thick wad of notes. She peeled one note off, paid the fine, and the gypsies were free.

"I am quite sure the money was not obtained honestly," Squire said. "It looked like hundreds of pounds in that bundle."

The world in which we were living was changing rapidly and I think Squire adjusted rather well. He had been brought up in a different world, but the number of incidents when I might have needed to tell Squire that he was too harsh with somebody decreased over the years.

Before and during the First World War there had been a distinct, almost feudal tradition that ruled our lives. It was a tradition of patronage by the land-owning class into which Squire had been born, and total dependence by us, the labourers, who toiled all day long. Each man to his own station, as it had been through the centuries.

In our little corner of England, however, it changed a little, at least for some people, after the war. Locally, a new middle class evolved.

Whilst it made very little difference to my life or those of most other labourers, farmers had benefited from prosperous years during and just after the war.

Mrs Calverley, the owner of Down Hall, was now in the process of selling her vast estate. During my childhood, she had on bitterly cold winter days sent a servant with a horse up to Matching Green to provide us with hot, thick nourishing soup. Huge soup tureens hung down on either side of the horse's saddle. We children would all rush up to the beautiful white mare, carrying our kettles and cans hoping that we would get to the front of the queue before the ladling out stopped as the tureens were emptied.

Mrs Calverley offered the freehold of many of her farms for sale to the tenant farmers, some of whom had accumulated enough money to buy the farms outright. Others were able to borrow the money for the purchase. To name but a few, Matching Hall, Stock Hall, Moat Hall, Hull Green, Rookwood Hall, Parville's and Kingston's were all bought by their tenants.

Now as owner-farmers, rather than humble tenant farmers, these men acquired a new social standing. Most did extremely well in the early years, but others, who had not been brought up with the strict discipline to run their farms like a business, failed over the ensuing years.

We could almost see it happen. They did not know what to do with their money -- or so it seemed to me. Spoilt by the good years and thinking that now they were prosperous farmers, almost akin to gentry, they spent furiously on smarter clothes, better maintained buildings and, above all, it became a 'social must' to own a motorcar.

Events, however, soon overtook them in the form of a deep farming recession. Farm labourer's wages were reduced from two pounds a week to twenty-nine shillings and sixpence after the deduction of ninepence for National Insurance. I wonder what today's labour force, not just in farming, but in any industry, would have to say about a twenty-five per cent reduction in wages?

This reduction did not affect me, however. Henry Lucking was still a struggling tenant farmer and my own wages had never reached these dizzying heights. I was still earning only eighteen shillings.

I was an avid newspaper reader and learned that the country was held in a vice by the spectre of unemployment. The workers, particularly in the industrial sector, suffered terribly during these years. Unemployment was as widespread as it proved to be lasting. Hunger marches and strikes followed, culminating in the General Strike in 1926.

I remember it well. Even though it did not affect our work, it did affect our plans for the weekend. Several of us had arranged to go to Leyton to watch the Australians play cricket. The strikers were a very militant lot and would have taken a very dim view of anybody who did not support them. But I did go.

A friend and I decided to take a chance and cycle the long way to Leyton. We were determined not to miss the chance of seeing the Aussies play. We made it there and back. I reckon the only reason we did so without being attacked was that my friend had been wise enough to wear his territorial sergeant's army uniform. But it was one hell of a devastating ride through the outskirts of London. Destruction was everywhere. The strikers had thrown milk churns into the middle of the road. We were absolutely leg-washed in milk riding through the street.

What a waste. There were people going hungry and these stupid people could overturn churns until the gutters flowed with milk. To me, this did not seem to be the right way to go about matters. My father-in-law, who was a policeman in the Metropolitan force at the time, told me some years later that the crime rate had risen alarmingly during that period. A state of anarchy had been feared. Fortunately the strike lasted only ten days.

Living at Little Laver Grange, Squire rented his old family home, Little Laver Hall, to a Miss Rolleston and her mother, a rector's widow from Stanford Rivers. Miss Rolleston was middle-aged and a very smart looking lady indeed. With the Rollestons came Arthur Cokin. He was their coachman, gardener and handyman. Whenever the Rollestons went out, Cokin would be there in his capacity of coachman, wearing a smart livery of beetle tail jacket, shiny black knee-high boots with a four-inch brown leather trim at the top, and a black silk top hat with a jaunty cockade tucked into its band. Generally, he drove a carriage pulled by a tandem of horses, but sometimes Miss Rolleston would drive herself in a dog cart or pony trap and Cokin would sit proudly on the dickey seat with his back to the passengers.

He looked immensely glamorous to us children. This was somebody who had obviously reached a very high position in service -- somebody to look up to. We would press our noses through the railings of the school yard marvelling at the spectacle of the Rollestons driving past -- and of course we never lost hope that Miss Rolleston might throw a few coins our way.

156

On Sundays, the Rollestons would attend morning service at Little Laver church, and evensong at St Edmunds on the Green. I always marvelled over how Miss Rolleston would step out of the church, put two fingers into her mouth in a most unladylike fashion and give a huge whistle. This was the signal for her two dogs to set off from Little Laver Hall and it was not very long before the large dogs came panting across the fields, overjoyed to meet their mistress and escort her home.

Physically, there was nothing much to Arthur Cokin. He was merely a bunch of bones in a jacket. He originally came from Bedfordshire and whilst I do not want to suggest that it is common to people of that county, he had the disconcerting habit of putting an 'H' wherever it did not belong. Some years after their arrival in Little Laver, I recall asking him: "How are you Mr Cokin?"

"H'all right. Can't h'afford to die, b'cause costs h'ermendous lot to bury you," came the reply. But despite his slight frame he was a extremely tough character, not easily fazed by anything. I recall his calmness being put to a particularly gruesome test when he accidentally cut off some of his fingers.

One of his duties was to make the home-brewed ale for his employer. The brew was checked regularly.

"Look h'at that, Perry," he said. "These buggers have drowned in my beer."

I looked over the edge of the barrel and saw a few dead mice floating on top of the brew.

"Never mind," Cokin shrugged, and plunged his hand into the liquid and scooped the mice out. "That'll add a bit of body," he added. "Never hurt anybody."

Then Cokin decided that the casket would be better standing on a shelf rather than on the floor. As he lifted it, the casket slipped and the fingers of his left hand got trapped under

157

the metal rim of the barrel. The index finger was severed at the knuckle and the middle and third finger a little lower.

Cokin swore profanely and furiously. Then he inspected the damage to his fingers, took out his penknife, laid the injured hand on the bench and 'tidied up' the wound by cutting straight across the jagged edges of his severed fingers.

"Now I'll need a bit of cogweg [cobweb]," he said, looking along the beams. Cobwebs were always abundant in the cellar and he soon had a handful of them wrapped around the bleeding stumps of his injured fingers. Then he proceeded to wrap the whole hand in a bit of none-too-clean cloth.

Yes, I know, it gives me goose pimples too even to think about it. I reckon there are not too many people today who could 'tidy up' their own fingers. It must obviously have been common knowledge amongst these old folk that cobwebs have healing qualities, and this incident certainly took place many years before penicillin was discovered.

I doubt if Cokin even bothered to inform his employer of the incident, and a couple of hours later he was back, cutting grass with a scythe.

After her mother died, Miss Rolleston left the parish and moved to Cambridge, but she was most kind to Mr Cokin who stayed behind in retirement. She helped him financially and Coachman's Cottage was built for him. She gave him a pony and generally made sure he was all right.

Cokin became a gnarled, little old man, and after his wife died, although personal cleanliness was not one of his priorities, I grew very fond of him. When Miss Rolleston had a bath installed in his house, he was most puzzled. At first he considered keeping the coal in it, but as it was indoors he made a concession and from there on kept his potatoes in it.

He was a character, the likes of which will never be seen again. He continued to work hard and gardened for three days each week at Little Laver rectory, a day at Waterman's End and occasionally at Little Laver Grange. I spent quite a bit of time with him. On summer evenings, I might help him cutting the road sides, or the churchyard, with a scythe. I did it for sheer fun. Most of the time he was very amusing company, and with my help Cokin was able to have a haystack for his pony.

One thing that he could not come to terms with at all was the radio. By then, most people would set their clocks by the time announced on the radio. If Cokin asked you the time, he would first make sure that you had not set your watch by the radio, because if you had, he would insist: "That's a dell sure mark that's wrong, because it has got to get there.

H'it can't be right." In his confident opinion, the radio time had to be wrong, because wherever it came from, it had to take time to get here and therefore would have lost time in the process. He would not be persuaded otherwise. Not that time was very important to him. He invariably had to wipe the clock face with his sleeve before he could read the time.

He was very opinionated in many other things. He told Squire during the Second World War: "If I was younger, I would join those h'airplane people."

"But Cokin you can't fly," Squire retorted. "You would have to be trained."

"Yes sir, I can. I can get in there and fly. Lots of people do it," Cokin replied stubbornly. "I'd gone up there and sorted them out."

Squire got rather irritated by the confident Cokin and his refusal to be corrected.

On another occasion, somebody had obviously discussed the latest war news with Cokin. By the time he relayed the hot piece of news to me, it sounded as follows: "They tell me Rotten Dam [Rotterdam] is in the war now. The Germans have h'invaded that country now. "The Japanese, he called 'Jampans'. The Jampans have done this or the Jampans

159

had done that, he would tell me. Cokin certainly could not read and this pronunciation was the closest he could get. God knows where the country of Jampan was in his mind.

Henry Lucking always said that Cokin was the only man he had ever known who could shear a sheep, milk a cow, clip a horse and make a wheelbarrow. But you needed a lot of strength to push any wheelbarrow made by Cokin.

In 1956, Mr Cokin fell ill and was taken to Epping Hospital. Whilst there for treatment, the nursing staff insisted on giving him a bath. He was horrified. He was ninety-seven years old and had never taken a bath before. To this day I am absolutely convinced that it killed him.

Chapter 14

I had been courting a young lady by the name of Winnie -- Miss Winifred Branch -- for some years. She was a lovely girl, very pretty and she had a lovely singing voice. Winnie called a halt to my endeavours when she learned that I had, in her opinion, paid rather a lot of attention to somebody else.

But after a couple of years of Winnie giving me the cold shoulder, I noticed that I was meeting Winnie more and more frequently on my way home, while she was returning at exactly the same time from the village having run an errand for the vicar's wife. Winnie worked as a housemaid for the Reverend and Mrs Davies at Little Laver rectory.

During one of our 'chance' encounters, Winnie and I arranged to meet at the rectory late at night. She had clearly forgiven me for having paid attention to other young ladies.

I walked down the Glebe, along a path between the field and the rectory grounds at the appointed time. This path would take me to the back of the house. I hung my hat on the gatepost and shone my torch three times as arranged. To my horror it was not Winnie that opened the back door and stepped out onto the path, but it was the vicar letting the dog out for his late night lifting-of-the-leg. Jib, a great big brute of a dog, rushed towards me at a rate of knots. With a speed that would have impressed the farm cat, I dashed down the path towards a lean-to shed. I grabbed the drainpipe and pulled myself up on to the roof. Jib came to a halt just below. His furious barking changed to a threatening growl. He was obviously none too fond of anybody prowling around 'his' grounds. Feeling very sheepish I sat on the roof, hoping, nay praying, that the vicar would not come to investigate. Luck was on my side, he just called the dog in.

After what I judged to be a suitable time, I scrambled off the roof, rearranged my dishevelled clothing and set off again.

I flicked the torch on and off three times and this time it was indeed Winnie who stepped out of the back door and pulled me into the kitchen.

"Have they gone to bed?" I asked.

"Yes they have been upstairs half an hour now."

I find it hard to describe the stunned sensation and leaden weight in my stomach when Mrs Davies' squeaky, high-pitched voice could be heard coming down the stairs: "Winnie".

The paralysis affecting both my brain and my legs did not last for long. Winnie pushed me into a cupboard, but I was too big and the door would not quite shut. Saucepan handles were sticking in my back, teapot spouts nuzzled my neck. I did not know what was behind me and what might come crashing down any moment. What t'hell am I going to do, I thought. My life flashed in front of my eyes: the inevitable consequences -- I (and Winnie) would get the sack. Squire would have nothing further to do with me -- I had disgraced him. I would be branded the rascal of the village.

"I think we ought to button this door up," Mrs Davies piped airily and pushed the door. I exhaled every bit of breath left in me, and she secured the door. God help me, what would have happened if she had opened the cupboard. Mrs Davies was a very slight woman, hardly bigger than a cat, and to be confronted by my six foot-plus frame in the cupboard...it does not bear thinking about.

After what I felt was an eternity, I heard her saying: "I am going up now." A thrill of thankfulness went through me, right down to the bone marrow. Winnie opened the door. I gasped and expelled myself, like a cork popping out of a bottle, from the cupboard. My luck held, nothing tumbled out after me, but my legs would barely hold me and I nearly landed on the floor. I was soaked with the cold perspiration of fear. Neither Winnie nor I had any appetite left for fraternising in the rectory kitchen after this. I legged it down the path as quietly and as quickly as I could. I was shaken to the bone, my pride in tatters.

But my troubles were not over yet. When I had nearly reached the road, I heard voices. My heart stopped. Two policemen were strolling along. The Matching Green policeman and the Morton policeman had met on their territorial border and were having a chat and a smoke. I hid in the bushes and waited for them to pass by. My heart restarted jerkily and I decided to take no further chances. I ran, like a rabbit pursued by a fox, right across the fields. My best brogue shoes and my blue mac were never quite the same again. Only when I reached Little Laver lodge, the best part of a mile from the rectory, did I start to breathe freely again. Reality suddenly struck me: my green pork pie hat was still hanging on the gatepost, and as far as I know it may still be there.

Thank heavens that Henry Lucking never found out. But he would have roared with laughter. It would have given him a good story to tell, all over the county, for months.

The Reverend Davies was the last of the residential parsons at Little Laver. Squire was immensely fond of him and thought him an excellent rector. On one occasion, I recall, Squire nearly spoiled their friendship. Reverend Davies had asked him to shoot some rabbits in his grounds as they were ruining his garden.

Squire was pleased to oblige. Whilst he was not a good all-round shot -- he would not have been able to hit a fox -- he was jolly good at shooting partridge and rabbits. And soon enough, we had shot a dozen rabbits, when suddenly a pheasant went up. Bang! Squire had fired and the pheasant came down. He plainly thought that he would please the Reverend Davies by providing him with a lovely pheasant for his table and when we gave it to him, he did indeed seem pleased.

"Well done, Squire," he piped. "What a beautiful bird. It's just like one I have walking around the garden."

I don't think he ever found out that Squire had shot his tame pheasant.

It was very unusual for Squire to shoot a pheasant at all, but he had clearly thought that he was doing the rector a favour. He never shot pheasants on his own land. He even brought in some very fancy varieties which strutted around the garden.

Whenever he had to give somebody a brace of pheasant as a gift, he would not have dreamt of shooting them on his own estate -- he sent to Harrods for them. His own birds were purely for visual enjoyment.

Reverend Davies, in his later years, went a bit funny, poor man. He always had to have somebody beside him at the lectern or he would have carried on right to the end of the book. He would go through the evensong and then would have married you and buried you all in one go. One of the parishioners would stand beside him and raise his hand gently at the appropriate moment to say: "Here endeth..."

Sometimes, the reverend even thought he was the bishop. It is sad that he suffered in this way, though he did nobody any harm and he had been a good parson to Little Laver.

Church was very much part of our lives and Winnie and I would occasionally walk to neighbouring churches to attend a service. Beauchamp Roding was one of our favourites. The vicar, the Reverend Howard, was something of an oddball. Standing tall and upright in the pulpit, he would take a deep breath and gesticulate expansively at the congregation. Then, with a huge effort, he would expel the air trapped in his lungs: "The d-d-d-devil is here, the d-d-d-devil is there, the d-d-d-devil is everywhere, the d-d-d-devil is in the pulpit."

Through my work for Squire in the shooting field I got to know another rather unusual clergyman, the Reverend Bernard Holme Vincent. He had become the rector of High Easter in 1916 and he was a wonderful shot. Squire was always pleased to include him in his shooting parties. Apart from his fine shooting I remember him for a couple of amusing eccentricities.

Reverend Vincent was a bachelor and a very handsome man. Many a mother must have thought him a suitable match for her daughter, and I am quite sure that some widows had their eye on him. He certainly was not short of lunch or dinner invitations.

However, Reverend Vincent managed to outsmart all his female flock. He remained a bachelor all his life, yet he would gladly accept their social invitations. He also used them to provide his own home cooking in the most crafty of ways.

His tailor had made him a special dinner jacket. The pockets were fitted with a waterproof lining.

During dinner he would find some excuse like:

"Dear Miss Wilson, would it be possible to have a little mustard to accompany this delicious piece of meat." And while his hostess left the room to obtain the item, he would deftly carve himself another large slice from the joint and tuck it in his pocket. Any other offerings on the table might finish up in another pocket.

Reverend Vincent was a wealthy parson. He certainly had no need to steal his food. Either he did it out of sheer devilment, which I would not put past him, or he suffered the same compulsion as modern day shoplifters.

When he reached home, so his servants told me, he would empty his pockets onto a plate and then label the contents -- Miss Wilson, lunch, lamb, Tuesday 19th, or Mrs Hepplethorpe, dinner, beef, Wednesday 20th. I somehow don't think his housekeeper had to cook many meals for him.

Many of the local farmers were well aware of the Reverend Vincent's great shooting abilities, but on occasions felt unable to invite him to their shoots. Possibly because they were intimidated by the very smart shoots Reverend Vincent frequently was seen to attend or because they wanted a bit of sport for themselves. Yet often when these local shots were taking place, the Reverend Vincent could be seen cycling up the path with his King Charles Spaniel sitting in a basket attached to the handlebars.

"I am sorry we could not include you, Reverend. We simply do not have enough birds this year," a farmer might call out to him, touching his cap most respectfully.

"Oh never mind, my good man," Reverend Vincent would reply. "Don't give it a thought. I am happy to stand just here and enjoy watching this drive. Then I will be on my way. I have parish business to attend to."

As the shooting party got on with their drive, Reverend Vincent would quietly push his bike along the path some distance behind them. His sporting eye would always detect a bird going down somewhere which the shooting party would have missed. Then, he whistled softly, and his well-trained spaniel would jump out of the basket and retrieve the bird. I have never known him to cycle home, with that impish grin on his face, without a brace or two hanging from the handlebars of his bike.

Everybody was dressed in shooting attire for his funeral, and standing at the graveside one of the guests muttered: "If somebody blew the whistle now [indicating that partridges had taken flight] now, he'd be out of that grave like a shot."

This is the only poaching rector I have ever known. But then, the only poacher I have actually caught in the woods turned out to be a policeman.

166

I do not, however, wish to give the impression that all clergymen, or policemen for that matter, were eccentrics. On the contrary, the rector of High Laver, the parish to which Perry Cottage belongs, was a most respectable and well-liked country parson. There was never even the slightest hint of scandal about the Reverend Claude H. Rowe. He was a large and tall man. He had been educated at Wellington and Oxford and spoke with a soft, cultured voice. Not one of those toff, grating accents, but with the voice of an educated man. He married fairly late in life, having met his wife, a nurse, in Ongar cottage hospital when he was admitted after an accident.

Despite his obviously wealthy and privileged upbringing, he was marvellous at looking after his impoverished parishioners. No matter how louse- and flea-infested their dwellings were, he would visit them. He would minister to his parishioners on Matching Green every single day. No matter what the problem, the rector was the first port of call. He was always there for you. If somebody wanted to get married, Reverend Rowe saw to it that they would find a home. At the other end of life, no sick or elderly person ever went without his care.

Granny held him in great respect.

"Boy, here comes the parson. Now I gotta drop he a curtsey," she would say whenever had was seen coming down our yard.

"That's the way I was brought up. We had to, in my days," she would explain when we told her that the rector did not expect a curtsey from an old, arthritic woman.

I often think that possibly today's Church could learn something from the likes of Reverend Rowe. If parsons were still held in the same high regard as he was, not necessarily for 'fire and brimstoning' their parishioners, but for caring and looking after their flocks as he did, the Church of England

167

might be in better shape. Parishioners are very shabbily treated by comparison today. No wonder the Church is losing its grip. Mind you, Claude Rowe most probably did not have to worry about the church commissioners losing eight hundred million pounds on property speculation. I cannot see how mismanagement of Church funds would have fitted in with his view of the Church.

He was a good sportsman too. He was captain of Matching Green cricket club and he was a beautiful player. People would come from many miles around to see him play.

I recall, though, that on one occasion he disappointed many who had come to Matching Green especially to see him. He cycled over, wearing his dog collar as usual and leant his bicycle against the cricket marquee. But it soon became apparent to the crowd that he had only come as a spectator.

This was a big blow to many of them. The star player was out of action. After all, cricket matches were very special occasions in a world were there was little other entertainment.

"Oh no! I couldn't possibly," the rector said, indicating that he was a little stiff. "I played for the Essex clergy yesterday. You know, Anno Domini is catching up with me."

"What?" I heard somebody ask indignantly. "Is the parson not playing today?"

"No," came the reply from a gnarled old man standing nearby. "He hurt himself playing dominoes."

The Reverend Claude Rowe was universally respected and we boys adored him. When he got on his bike to leave the Green to go home to High Laver rectory, we would hop, skip and trot behind him for a mile down the road.

On the first occasion when I had been chosen to play away for the first eleven of Matching Green cricket club, he took me along in a pony trap which he had hired. I felt

168

tremendously elated and very proud. Sixteen years old and I was good enough to be chosen to play in the first eleven. I was to play in a team together with farmers, a stockbroker and the parson. I was very proud indeed. Before this I had been a scorer, a twelfth man, or just an onlooker.

The game was played at Rickling Green. I held two catches and got seven runs not out and I walked on air for days.

"I am delighted. I am delighted," Reverend Rowe exclaimed.

Yet on another occasion when I thought I had saved our cricket team's bacon, he pulled me up sharply.

We had been playing at Cloghams Green. We were getting nowhere. The rector was out and most of the other batsmen were out. Basil Gingell, vice captain of Matching Green cricket club, approached me.

"Go in, young Perry. Give them some stick," he said. "I know you can do it."

I went in and the ball hit the middle of the bat very nicely. Good. I was timing it right. I hit two sixes over the willow trees, several boundaries, and was caught out beautifully right in the pavilion door. Glorious! What an innings! I can't quite remember how many runs I made, but quite a lot.

Triumphantly, I returned to the pavilion only to be met by the captain, Reverend Claude Rowe.

"I don't like it," he said. "I don't like it."

"This is more liking watching a game of golf," he expanded indignantly, and he took me over to the practice nets which were adjacent to the pavilion. He proceeded to bowl a series of balls to show me how it was done.

"You will have to play cricket properly," he explained. "Not with golf shots or I would rather see our team lose."

"You have to play with your left elbow up to be able to play the ball into the ground," he told me sincerely. "You hit far too many cross bat swipes."

A very amused Cloghams Green team and the spectators looked on as the player who had won the game for Matching was given a public lesson in the finer points of cricket.

Fred Perry

Reverend Rowe was one of the first people to get a motor car. Willie Walden, owner of the bicycle shop, had been the very first owner on Matching Green. We had watched Willie's car huff, puff and smoke around the Green, rarely making it without breaking down. It made so much noise that the horses got frightened and would gallop around their paddocks or across the Green. But Willy's car was secondhand and the rector had acquired a brand new, shining 'bull-nosed' Morris. It could sit two people in the front and it had a dickey seat in the back which would seat one or, at a push, two people. The dickey seat faced to the back, but that didn't matter one bit. It was still a thrill to ride in it.

"Would you like to come to Brentwood with me to see Essex play," the rector asked me one day.

I was over the moon. Would I like to see Essex play? They were my heroes. Of course I would like to see them play. And so we went in his lovely car to Brentwood.

I feel very lucky to have known this man. He was a lovely parson and he remained a good friend to me over the years. The rector retired from active cricket, but remained a firm supporter of Matching Green cricket club and was its treasurer. To help the cricket club funds, we would hold little dances or whist drives. Whist was a very popular game and people would walk for miles in the hope of a prize.

I was usually entrusted with taking the proceeds over to the treasurer.

"Oh do come in. I am delighted," he would say. I spent many an evening at the rectory with him and his wife chatting about cricket, village or current affairs.

Chapter 15

Often the rector would ask me when I intended to get married. I was well into my twenties and he obviously thought it was time for me to settle. I was never quite sure if he had heard that I had taken a good many girls out and was worried on that account or if his comments were general.

It was quite true, I had taken many a girl out. I very much liked dancing, sometimes we went to church together or I might take them to whist drives. But I did not deserve the rakish reputation I had somehow acquired and I do not think that too many mothers were worried about me taking their daughters out. I think the reputation was created by my envious peers. I was a tall, reasonably presentable young man who liked the company of women. Now as I speak at ninety years old, I can only tell you that I am still tall. But in those days I was a good-looking fellow and not ready to tie the knot yet. On the whole I behaved very properly towards the girls. If they were forward, I simply did not want to take them out as I automatically assumed that I was not the only one getting their attention.

Mind you, girls then were very much more demurely dressed than they are today. If you had wanted to be somewhat naughty, you might have needed a bookmark to find your way around all those voluminous skirts: find the bookmark to know where you had got to last week. If they had worn clothes which leave little to the imagination, as young girls do today, I might have been married somewhat earlier.

Granny was never particularly concerned.

· "As long as you don't go to them haycarter girls," was her only comment. "God help you if I hear that you have been near them. Ma'k ma words!" This is where she drew the line.

These girls were prostitutes the haycarters brought back on the haycart from their journeys of delivering hay to

London. The girls would ply their trade and sleep in the hay barn and after a few days would catch a lift back to London with the haycarters. But Granny had no need to worry about me on this account. The haycarters' girls held no attraction for me.

Once, as a very young man I had taken a girl to a whist drive and I had been the winner of the first prize -- two herrings. There I was, clutching my herrings, and with no newspaper or bag to wrap them in. I was faced with the prospect of having to walk the girl home clutching two slippery herrings. I am afraid the herrings won and I went straight home. How many young men can claim that supper took priority over a pretty girl.

Then there was Ivy, the young girl who had caused a great deal of mischief to my friendship with Winnie. Ivy worked with my mother for the Noble-Jones family in Buckinghamshire. She was a pretty and bubbly girl and to give her a treat, Mother had asked her to come along home for her annual holiday.

"Why don't you take Ivy out for a walk," Mother suggested. "Show her some of the countryside." I duly took Ivy out for a country walk, but, oh dear, she was all over me. Not long after we had left the village behind us, she was tangled around my neck. She was very forward indeed.

Ivy had taken a real shine to me and I can't altogether say that this was reciprocated. Nevertheless, one evening Mother gave me hell for being out late with Ivy.

"Where have you been so long," she demanded to know. "Walking! Pah! I know that Ivy. You just watch yourself."

I was getting somewhat angry at this. After all I had not asked for Ivy's attentions.

"Well if you knew what Ivy is like," I retorted, "why did you bring her here?"

Needless to say, Winnie had heard meanwhile that I had been seen out walking with another girl on several occasions and had not liked it one little bit. Then Ivy's letters started to arrive at Little Laver Grange. I was getting into a right muddle. I did not know what to do about Ivy. How could I put a stop to all of this?

I went to see Mrs Allen, Squire's housekeeper. She had always been very kind to me. She would, I was sure, understand and help me solve this sticky problem. And so she did. She helped me write a letter to Ivy, but by this time Winnie had had enough and told me where to go -- which was nowhere near her.

Mrs Allen had taken me in hand when I first started working for Squire. She had been very kind and ensured that I learned some standards of cleanliness. She would send away for little samples of toothpaste and give them to me with precise instructions on how to use them. Or she would see to it that my hair was combed and cut regularly. When I became a little older, she advised me on what clothes to purchase. She, in fact, turned me into the presentable young man I became. There were many other things she taught me, including how to treat girls. Poor old Granny could not have helped me. Granny knew little of this new world and my mother was never around for long enough to teach me anything.

Anyhow, Mother was a very stern and disapproving woman. I never got very close to her and I certainly never quite understood her. Mother, during her two weeks' annual leave, would tell me off if I did not look right or had done something she did not approve of. But she never sat down patiently, as did Mrs Allen, to explain. Possibly she had been in 'smart' service for so long that she had forgotten that behaviour has to be learned.

Mother was what in today's language would be called a very poor communicator. Even in later years, when she lived with me and my wife, I never got to know her. She wouldn't even discuss my father with me as other mothers might have done.

'Mother'
Ellen Eliza Perry, 1878 - 1970

"What was he like? Was he handsome? Was he clever? Was he nice?" Questions any child might ask about their dead father would go unanswered. I only saw a photograph of my father once -- when it accidentally fell out of Mother's handbag.

I picked it up before she could stop me. I saw the picture of a smart army officer standing in full parade uniform, plumed helmet under his left arm and holding his horse with his right hand. He looked very smart. Mother then told me that he had gone to France with his regiment, the First Life Guards, and had been one of the very first casualties of the First World War.

With that explanation, she snatched the photograph back from me, put it back in her handbag and snapped the clasp firmly shut.

Henry Lucking was also keen to know what my intentions regarding marriage were.

"Are you going to get married, Freddie John?" he asked.

175

"The Leather Bottle is empty. You could have that." The Leather Bottle had been a rowdy pub before my time, but was now one of the farm cottages.

"Not if I can help it, sir," I smugly replied. "I don't want to get married yet. And anyhow we have got our own place. I wouldn't leave Granny on her own."

"Well, never let it be said that I told you to get married," Mr Lucking grinned at me. It was really a kind offer to point out that I might be able to rent the Leather Bottle cottage. Often it was the lack of a house which stood in the way of a young couple getting married. And having my own house, rather than living in a tied cottage, has always stood me in good stead. It gave you much greater independence. It left you free to consider changing your employer without having to consider the accommodation. Not that it ever happened to me. I did not change employment all my life, but I have seen many a labourer fall out with the farmer, lose their job and have their families homeless in the same day.

In the summer of 1932, a new family had settled in Matching Green. They moved into Elm House on the Green.

For most of my life, Elm House had been a convalescence home with the patients regularly wheeled out into the front garden overlooking the Green. It was run by two sisters, Nurse Wells and Sister Wells, and they were often called to help whenever there had been a calamity in the village.

Before that time, the painter, Augustus John, had lived there, together, so the older villagers said, with his wife and his mistress. Their housekeeper was often found in the Chequers pub. In those days, when women were almost never seen inside the pub, she would stagger the few steps from the pub to the safety of the tall wrought iron fence at the front of Elm House, grab a fence bar and steadily pull herself along until she reached the door to the house.

Augustus John was reputed to have been quite a womaniser. Many of the village girls had modelled for him, but in later years I often heard the older village women comment: "T'at on' mixed with t'at painter chap." If out of sheer envy or from disapproval, I was never quite sure.

The beautiful etchings below [Augustus John c.1903/4] are of the 14 year old Lucy Claydon, who later became my Uncle George's wife.

The new family, by contrast, seemed to be most respectable. It was a retired policeman from London, his wife and children. Their name was Tappin, gossip informed me. From the cricket ground, where I spent much of my free time, I had a fine view of Elm House and was able to observe their comings and goings.

177

Mr Tappin was a tall upright man. He looked exactly like a policeman ought to look. But I was particularly interested in the daughter of the house. I had seen her walking her dog and she looked very attractive and had a smashing pair of legs.

Mr Tappin, Elsie's father

One day, during cricket practice, I found the Tappin's beautiful springer spaniel playfully bounding up to me, and behind it, calling her dog, was Miss Elsie Tappin. I made a great deal of fuss of the spaniel in the hope that this would have a favourable impression on the owner. This was quite easy as the young spaniel, whose name I learned was Gerry, was a lovely dog.

Thereafter, on several occasions, Gerry found me on the Green. He clearly liked to give his owner the slip and do a spot of exploring for himself, possibly checking out the local bitch population. I got friendly with the dog and as planned, became acquainted with the owner. Strictly speaking, Miss Tappin did not own Gerry. The dog belonged to her Uncle Fred, and she was only looking after it.

Miss Tappin had worked as a dressmaker in London's exclusive Bond Street and was not altogether pleased with her father's desire to retire to the country. She was twenty-one years old, but as I learned later, her father was not to be disobeyed. She had dark hair, waved gently over the forehead and modishly cut to shoulder length. I am sure that she was the most stylishly dressed girl in the village.

Miss Elsie Tappin

There wasn't a great deal for her to do in Matching Green and she did not much like the fact that there were no street lights. The darkness of a night in the country was not something she was used to.

After I had met her a few times, she kindly agreed to accompany me to a whist drive, and on her father's instructions I brought her back home again at a very reasonable hour. By now I had learned that Mr Tappin was a strict man. I have never known anybody who looked, sounded and behaved more like a policeman. In his deep, slow voice he said: "Make sure you have Elsie back here by ten o'clock," whilst looking at me as if to say: I am not sure about you -- yet. I'll keep an open mind -- for the moment.

Occasionally we went on a bicycle ride together, but that was not a great success. Elsie did not care for cycling. She had only recently learned to cycle, after her father had decided to move to the country. In London she had not needed this skill and she never took to it. Long country walks became our preference.

179

Fred and Elsie Perry
17th April 1933

We were married in Little Laver Church on Easter Monday, 1933. Elsie was twenty-two years old, I was twenty-seven.

Uncle Fred Tappin gave Gerry to Elsie as a wedding present. Henry Lucking, totally out of character gave me five pounds. I have never known him to give anybody five pounds.

Squire, a bachelor himself, did not generally approve of women: "Designing hussies, most of them," he would say. "I am sure they ruined our family." Squire's grandfather had been married four times; his father three times and Squire himself had been subjected to two stepmothers. His experience of women had made him a irredeemable bachelor. Yet if I insisted on getting married, he felt that Elsie was an excellent choice: a policeman's daughter.

For me, getting married to Elsie was the best thing I ever did. She has been a marvellous wife to me. And I think that she was terribly brave to take me on. To leave her comfortable life at Elm House, marry me and live at Perry Cottage. Her ways were so very different to Granny's. I don't think they had anything in common at all, but she took on Granny as well and looked after her. I have been a very lucky man indeed.

You see, you have to remember that Perry Cottage was not always the comfortable home it is now. It was many years before we could afford to put in floors, heating and a bathroom.

As a wedding present, Elsie and I received our very first radio. It was a marvellous new radio, powered by an accumulator -- the latest in radio technology. Once a week, we would take the accumulator to the local garage, leave it overnight and for sixpence it would be charged up. The BBC had started broadcasting in 1922, but before the accumulator radio, the only radios had been the crystal set.

A crystal set would have to be very finely tuned with a 'cats whisker' and one could only listen through a pair of headphones. Our lovely new set had a loudspeaker and could be heard by all in the room. A wonderful wedding gift indeed.

But my absolute favourite wedding present was Gerry. He was a magnificent, rather tall, liver and white springer spaniel, though whilst I was delighted to have 'my own' dog, Granny never quite got used to having him around the house. Her unease grew after one particular occasion when Gerry had been left in her charge and apparently had nearly jumped out of the upstairs window to follow Elsie and me. Granny caught him just in time and closed the window. But Gerry continued to hit the window catch with his paw and Granny was convinced that he would either hurt his foot or succeed in breaking the glass and so jump out of the window.

He was quite a powerful dog and Granny told us that he had almost knocked her over coming down the stairs. Granny, who by now was most frustrated and angry with Gerry, opened the

Elsie with Gerry (left) and Prim (right)

181

door and let him go. We found him hurtling after us a few miles down the road on our way to Otes pond.

We went to Otes pond regularly as the owner had given me permission to shoot ducks there. "Shoot as many as you like Fred," he said, "just leave me a pair hanging in the barn. No more than a pair. I have better things to do than pluck bloody ducks."

I never shot more than half a dozen, but it was lovely sport and delicious dinner. One evening, a neighbour came along with me for the shooting. It was already quite late in the season and the birds were getting a little bit more wily. We took our respective positions and Gerry sat by my feet anxiously waiting for me to shoot so that he could rush off and retrieve my kills. Some time passed and while Jack already had several ducks lying by his feet, I had yet to fire my first shot. Gerry's head turned and he looked up at me with a mournful expression. Shortly afterwards, I noticed him skulking away. What is it old mate, I thought. Have you had enough of this? Are you bored with just sitting around?

To my utter amazement, I saw Gerry returning after a short while carrying a dead duck in his mouth. Slowly and not meeting my astonished gaze he slunk back to my side and deposited the bounty by my feet, just as he would have done if he had retrieved a duck. But in contrast to a normal retrieve, he was very subdued, as if I was not meant to notice the sudden appearance of the duck at my feet.

My neighbour later filled me in on what happened. Apparently, Gerry had turned up by his side and sat down. "He looked at me with that beautiful face," he said. "Why did you leave your master, Gerry?"

"The very next moment I knew why he was here," Jack explained. Gerry grabbed one of my ducks and hightailed it back over to you."

Gerry obviously couldn't bear to see me going without -- and if I couldn't shoot one, well, he just had to take matters into his own hands.

Whoever said that dogs can't think? This was a carefully thought out manoeuvre and quite obviously intended to spare my tender feelings. Gerry was taking care of his own.

A few years later, we also acquired one of Gerry's daughters and we named her Judy. She was rather a lovely little thing and totally dominated by Gerry.

One Friday evening, a friend, the gamekeeper Frank Gooday, came by to ask me to join them at Enville's for shooting the next day. Pointing at Gerry who was sitting by my feet, he said: "Why not leave Gerry at home tomorrow. Bring Judy. It'll give her a chance." So we agreed that I would bring only Judy next morning.

As I was getting ready for bed that evening, I noticed that Gerry was missing. At first I thought that he had just popped outside to uncross his legs, but it soon became apparent that Gerry could not be found. Elsie and I searched high and low. We called him and scoured the Green for him, but finally we had to admit defeat. Gerry would come back when he was ready to. It was not the first time this had happened. Gerry went absent once in a while to visit a lady of his choice.

Next morning, there was still no sign of Gerry and I got ready to go off for the day's shooting. I put a box on the back of my bicycle and tucked Judy in it. This was her usual place whenever she came along with me. Gerry, who was much stronger and had longer legs, would usually run alongside.

Today, it was just Judy and I who cycled off to meet the others at Little Laver Grange. Of course it had not been my intention to bring Gerry along today, but my mind would have been considerably easier if I had known where he was. Regardless of my telling myself that he was out courting, I was a little worried.

But there was no need for my concern -- Gerry had outsmarted us. He was sitting in the porch at Little Laver Grange waiting for me. He looked at me almost contemptuously and his entire body language seemed to be saying: Did you really think you could get away with leaving me behind? You will have to be smarter than that.

I don't want to give Gerry human qualities, but he was one of the most amazingly clever dogs I have ever known.

One evening after work, instead of walking along the road in the direction of home, I took the shortcut across the field and through the Spinney. I came out of the wood, and was heading towards Waterman's End, when I noticed a little smoke coming out of Mrs Lucking's chicken house. There was somebody smoking in there. Rather puzzled, I sauntered over to have a look and to my astonishment found my employer, the farmer Henry Lucking, sitting on a box in the chicken house, merrily smoking his pipe, with his gun standing beside him.

"What are you doing here, sir," I enquired in amazement.

"The bloody fox has been taking my bloody chickens," he replied. "The missus has asked me to take care of him."

I could quite see why Mrs Lucking would be upset about the fox taking her chickens from the little meadow. All farmers' wives relied on the eggs and the cow's milk for their pin money. Yet I had to chuckle at Mr Lucking's' antics of trying to get the better of old Charlie.

"You don't really think the fox is going to come anywhere near you, sir?" I stated.

"And why bloody well not?" he asked.

"Well, sir, I could smell the pipe and see the smoke, and I am quite sure that the fox's nose is a darn sight better than mine," I explained.

"Well, if you know so bloody much about it, why don't you do something," he retorted.

Leaving Mr Lucking still muttering and sitting on his box, I continued on my way home, smiling to myself. I was quite sure that part of the reason he was sitting there was that he wanted to get out of the house. His wife would surely have found another task for him to do -- like washing eggs. I had often seen Mr Lucking standing in the harness room at Waterman's End, with his great big hands gently washing the eggs, lest his wife would chastise him for having broken one.

A few nights later, I decided to take Gerry and my gun down to the Spinney to give the dog some exercise.

"Go on then! Go on then, Gerry, have a good run," I encouraged him, knowing full well that his rushing around the Spinney wouldn't do any harm. I was walking up the rise that would take me out of the Spinney on the Waterman's End side, when I heard a 'splash, splash' through puddles in the undergrowth. I turned around, expecting Gerry to have caught up with me. The recognition flashed through my mind: Hold on a moment, that's not my dog, that's a fox.

Charlie has beaten me, I thought. He had nearly crossed the rise and would imminently be out of the reach of my gun. Damn it, I cursed, and aimed. I swung past his brush and pulled the trigger. Bang!

"Christ," I thought. "If I had seen you a moment earlier, I would have got you. Well, never mind, Charlie, you got away this time."

After a short while Gerry came hurtling past me, having taken the fox's scent. He jumped back when he got to the bushes where I had last seen the fox.

I walked over and to my surprise there lay the fox -- dead. I had managed to time it right after all. I picked him up by his brush and his front legs and walked across the meadow to Waterman's End.

I knocked on the kitchen door and Mr Lucking opened it. He was dressed in the blue serge suit that I normally only saw him wear in church. He had obviously changed his working clothes in readiness for supper.

"Is this what you have been looking for, sir," I asked, holding up the fox.

He turned around and called out to his wife: "Siss, give him a pound, he's got the fox." He walked back into the house, without another word, while I heard Mrs Lucking nagging: "What did he do that for? Why did you ask him? Why couldn't you have done it yourself?"

After quite a long while she came to the door and gave me the one pound reward.

I thanked her and walked over to the brewhouse. Poor man, I thought, whilst counting my blessings. Mrs Lucking gave him a hard time over everything. He did not get much peace at home. From the brewhouse I extracted an old sack, put the fox in it and carried him the mile over to Little Laver Grange where Albert Clarke the stockman skinned him for me. No good wasting a good pelt.

Bond's of Chelmsford made it into a fur for Elsie. Elsie's brother was a policeman in Chelmsford and he helped me to arrange it. At the next opening meet of the hunt, Elsie was seen with a smart fox fur around her neck, which I thought highly amusing. She didn't, however, wear it for long. She said it did not suit her at all. A bit disappointing.

Chapter 16

One Saturday morning, Mr Lucking had gone to Chalk Pit field, which that year had been planted with wheat. A lot of surface water had collected on the field and we generally cleared this by using a one-furrow horse plough to create a channel for the water to run off. Mr Lucking was very good at keeping his fields well drained. At lunchtime the horsekeeper was sent over to tell Mr Lucking that his lunch was ready and that his wife had said that he was late. Henry Lucking was lying down in the field, his filled but unlit pipe beside him. He had fallen down dead from a heart attack.

Bill Furze, the neighbouring farmer, walked over and told me that my governor had died. Oh dear me, I was sad to hear that news, if not altogether surprised. Mr Lucking had suffered several milder heart attacks before and he had told me that Dr Shields had warned him about his pipe. Whenever Dr Shields had given him a pep talk about Mr Lucking's pipe smoking -- he was never without it -- he might ease up for the next twenty-four hours and chew some liquorice, but he had said to me often: "Without my pipe, I might as well be dead." I had a tremendous fondness for that big jovial man. He was a mere sixty years old when he died.

Mr Lucking's body was carried back home to Waterman's End and a grave was prepared for him in Little Laver churchyard -- alongside the old horse pond. Henry Lucking had been so very fond of his horses that I think he might have been pleased to know that his horses would come to drink right beside his grave, just as I had often taken joy from the snorting and whinnying horses as they came up to the fence whenever I walked to church. It was a lovely sound. They knew their people.

Two horses were brassed up, hitched to the best wagon and Mr Henry Lucking went on his last journey along the road which he must haven taken every day of his life, to Little Laver churchyard right next to Little Laver Grange. Our three horsekeepers were dressed in their best black suits. Two of them walked beside the horses and the third one, carrying a whip, walked ahead.

Henry Lucking would have liked to have seen his horses and their keepers so beautifully turned out. Farming with horses had been his passion, and indeed we had always had at least a dozen beautiful ones. Whilst he had occasionally been forced to get a contractor with a tractor in when things got a bit behind, he was of the firm conviction that farming with good horses was the only way to success in agriculture. "They [the tractors] won't last, you know," he had said to me once. "They will never replace a good horse." Little did he know. But I am happy in the knowledge that Henry Lucking was able to work with these wonderful horses during all his life.

Squire had asked me to make the freshly dug grave a little more friendly looking by laying a net around it and placing masses of flowers on it. After all, a hole in the bare earth looks very stark and cold -- and possibly very distressing for the widow. Squire, I thought, was very caring and considerate in this request, but I was given an awfully hard time for my efforts by Mrs Lucking a few days after the funeral. How dare I interfere in her funeral arrangements? I pointed out to her that she should have known that I could not have and would never have, at my own instigation, raided Squire's garden until it was virtually bare and laid the flowers around the graveside. Servants or labourers did not use their initiative in such matters -- they were told what to do. However, I never did mention to her that Mr Lucking had always told me that he did not want to be buried at Little Laver, but rather at Magdalen Laver with the rest of his family.

Henry Lucking had been a good farmer, even if he kept his farm account chalked up on the barn door. He had treated the inside of the big double barn doors as if they were a huge blackboards. He might swear at you one moment, but the next he would be a bundle of fun. Like the occasion when a contractor, Fred Hoy, came to cut a hayrick. To see a good haycutter, or hay tier as they were known, was like watching a work of art. The haycutter's big knife would cut a corner out of the rick, take the first neat bundle off and place it on the press. A clock weight hanging on the side of the press would register the weight. Thereafter the lid of the press was lowered and the hay pressed into a neat, compact bundle. Two strings would be fastened around it before it was ready for us to load onto the wagons for delivery to London.

"I want to have a word with you, Hoy," Mr Lucking called out as he approached.

"I am too busy to talk to you, Master," replied Fred Hoy.

"In that case," Mr Lucking said, and he took a bundle of hay, carefully positioned it on the press and sat himself on top of it, grinning, "you'll have to make the time now."

A good hay tier could tell you by looking at the rick what the tonnage would be. It was truly an art. My friend and childhood neighbour, Charlie Holgate was a good hay tier. Hay tiers were paid by the ton of hay they had cut, pressed and tied and often they had to travel long distances to the next job. Charlie often says: "I have travelled all over Essex on my bicycle to tie hay, for three shillings and sixpence per week.

The Holgates were very poor indeed. Charlie's father had gone into the army during the First World War in the hope that he would be able to provide a little better for his family, but had been killed. His wife Ede, had to try and feed the family herself. She worked extremely hard, took in washing and undertook any job she could get.

189

I remember her calling the children in from playing in the yard.

"Come along, dears," she called, in her pleasant sing-song voice. "Time for your tea. We have only got one egg, but I'll cut it up so you can share it between the four of you."

To bring up thirteen children without a husband was no mean feat, and so when Ede, had been approached by a local hay tier, she had been delighted.

"Will your boy come and work for me, Ede?" he asked.

"He has got to work for somebody, dear," she had replied, shrugging her shoulders.

"I'll pay what he yarns [earns]," was the hay tier's reply, and the deal was done. Charlie became an assistant hay tier. Often he had to travel such great distances on his bicycle, that there was little time to earn his tonnage money. But, it sure as hell made him a master of bicycling. To this day, in his eighties now and after a hip replacement operation, you rarely see Charlie around Matching Green unless he is on a bicycle. "To ride is easier for me than to walk," he will say.

Farming at Little Laver Grange and at Waterman's End changed swiftly and dramatically after Mr Lucking's death.

Not long after his funeral, Mrs Lucking called me over. "Fred," she said, "you will remember that my husband always wanted you to have his gun." I did indeed remember as he had told me so on many occasions. "Freddie John when I die you will get my gun," he would say. On one occasion, I recall, he even called across to his wife: "Siss, did you hear that? Remember when I die I want Freddie John to have my gun."

Well, she did remember: "Fred, he did so want you to have his gun," she told me. "The sale of his possessions is tomorrow. Please come and bid for it."

"W'hat! Squire huffed and puffed when he heard this. "Don't buy it, Fred. I advise you not to buy it. That penny pinching hussy." And I didn't.

190

(left to right) Squire's sister, Mrs C Douglas, Squire,
Jane Lucking (sitting in the bathchair) and Fred Perry

Mrs Jane Lucking, Squire's old nanny and the mother of Henry Lucking, did not survive her son for very long. She died the same year and is buried beside him at Little Laver.

"What a lovely surprise for Henry when he meets his mother in heaven," an elderly Lucking relative commented at the funeral. I am personally not so sure. Henry might have been quite pleased to be out from under his mother's clutches. She had dominated him all his life. Three weeks had not been a long respite.

Chapter 17

On Lady's Day, 25th March 1935, Squire took on a new tenant -- Mr Thomas Glasse.

Mr Glasse and his family moved into Waterman's End and soon the farm changed totally. He was a more up-to-date farmer, who had arrived with his own tractor and tractor driver. He selected the farm workers he wanted to keep. He was very apologetic to the ones he had to let go, but a modern mechanised farm did not need as many hands.

I stayed on. Then one day, Mr Glasse asked me if I wanted to have a go at driving the tractor. He explained it to me and I sat down in the driver's seat. Mr Glasse was standing beside me on the draw bar, taking me through the functions of the tractor. I must have performed reasonably well, because the next time I looked round, he had jumped off and was walking away. Thus, I became a 'modern' agricultural worker, even though I occasionally missed the sight of the heaving horse's flanks in front of me.

Mr Glasse was a very different man to Henry Lucking -- truly as different as chalk and cheese. Mr Glasse had been a military man and he spoke like one. Just like Squire's, his voice sounded like a rifle shot. I liked working for Mr Glasse and continued to do so, and later for his son Graham, until I retired in 1981 after sixty-four years of working the same patch of wonderful Essex.

The Glasses hired a new tractor driver shortly after their arrival. Jack Crane was a tall man and his hair was carefully parted in the centre. Quite a reasonable looking fellow. He was as strong as an ox and worked all the hours God made. One could not find a better worker -- if Crane had the mind to work -- or a better mate.

Nevertheless, Crane could be quite difficult get on with. He liked to be the boss and this did not go down well with everybody. It did not bother me overly much. I had developed my own way of dealing with him. If he wanted to be boss -- he was the older man -- so be it. It did not hurt my pride. If I just worded things carefully when making suggestions, Crane did everything you wanted whilst thinking it had been his idea all along.

One day a lorry driver, who had come to Little Laver Grange to collect some corn, approached me.

"I hear you have Jack Crane working here now," he said.

"Yes, what of it," I replied.

"Oh dear, Jack is a card," the lorry driver replied. "He is a crafty one, that one."

"Did he ever tell you how he poached the young pheasant stock from the Tufnels at Great Waltham?" he continued.

We all knew by this time that Crane was a bit of a rascal and I was therefore very interested to hear the story.

Apparently, Crane had been poaching the young pheasant stock from the Tufnel estate and selling them on to somebody else. Two nights running he had got away with raiding the birds, but on the third night the local policeman was waiting for him.

"Caught you red-handed you blackguard. What is your name," the policeman asked, while unbuttoning his top pocket to get his notebook and pencil.

At this point, Crane saw his opportunity. He grabbed the policeman's helmet and flung it as far as he could over the nearest hedge. While the policeman was looking round to see what had happened, Crane scampered.

The next morning his buyer and accomplice in this crime, asked Crane:

"What shall we do? Does he know your name?"

"Not bloody likely. I took this while I was at it," Crane said, whipping the policeman's notebook out of his pocket.

When I told my father-in-law, Harry Tappin, a retired policeman, about it later, he said: "It's hardly surprising. The policeman could hardly report the crime without his notebook."

"I would rather say that he kept quiet about it," he added. "For a policeman to lose his notebook is asking for trouble with his sergeant."

This is not to say that father-in-law saw the funny side of the story. He did not, as he strongly disapproved of law-breaking in any shape or form. I rather gather that he had been a very good policeman. He certainly looked and sounded the part.

Elsie always told me that before her father had retired to Matching Green, whenever somebody came to call for him at their house, he would put his helmet on before he did anything else. The helmet, apparently, hung on the post at the foot of his bed. If anybody called for him in the middle of the night, the upstairs window would open.

"Yes. Who is it?" Harry Tappin would boom.

The caller would be confronted by the view of Tappin leaning out of the window in pyjamas - and with his helmet on.

Squire did not like Crane at all. His facial expression would register real distaste when he spoke about him.

"I have seen too many of his kind, what!" he would say. "He has got one of those long dogs." By this he meant a greyhound. His concern was that the dog would go after the hares. Squire disapproved of hare coursing.

He was right to disapprove, I learned later. Not on account of the dog, but I learned that Crane would set off with his gun hidden down his trouser leg. Crane was well aware that if he was seen with the gun, somebody would report it to Squire. Crane was undoubtedly bagging some of Squire's birds.

Squire would have been horrified had he known that I

sometimes went for a drink with Crane. I never wanted to -- and never did -- have anything to do with Crane's dubious activities and dealings, but we did become pals. If I had ever got into trouble, I would have been pleased to have had him by my side.

Mr Glasse seemed to close both eyes to Crane's antics. Crane would pinch a bag of corn here or a bale of hay there. I saw him do it, and I am quite sure that if I knew, Mr Glasse knew. I guess that Crane was just too good a man on the farm to let go. For all I know, Crane might have had a talking to from Mr Glasse.

Laughingly, Mr Graham Glasse told me many years later, after his father had retired and he had taken over the reins: "I am quite sure the man should really be in prison, but I am sure he would have pinched everything in there by now, and they would be pleased to be rid of him."

"But he is a loveable rogue," he added.

Old Crane was as strong as an ox and a tremendously hard worker, and I can fully understand why Mr Glasse put up with him. He was a real original.

Mr Glasse had asked me to go along with the horsekeeper to Magdalen Laver and help him bring a bull over to Waterman's End. We had a dozen heifers in 'Daniel's Mead', which he wanted covered. As we had no suitable cart ourselves, he had arranged that we could borrow a cattle truck.

I hunted through the nettles and found the cattle cart. We hitched the horse to it and were ready to load the bull. What we had anticipated to be a tricky enterprise -- getting the bull into the cart -- proved as easy as pie. The cattle cart looked somewhat like an old-fashioned horse box with two doors at the rear allowing access for the cattle and a small observation door at the front. The farmer, owner of the bull, strolled into the cart and climbed out again through the observation door. The bull simply followed him in and we closed the doors. Easy!

We brought the bull back and waiting for us were Mr Glasse and Crane -- our reception committee. We opened the doors of the cattle cart expecting the bull to walk out. But the beast just stayed there. No amount of coaxing helped. The bull moaned and groaned, but he would not come out.

"I'll get the bloody bugger out," Crane exclaimed.

"Don't you go in there, Jack," I said. "You'll get hurt."

Crane took no notice of my warning and he opened the little observation door and climbed in.

Crash! Through the wooden side of the cart first came Crane followed by an angry bull. Crane turned over several times like a shot rabbit, but fortunately the bull had by this time spotted the heifers which had gathered to watch the commotion.

Crane got up with a grin on his face: "I told you I would get the old bugger out."

We asked him if he had hurt himself, but I know that if he had he would not have told us.

"There is a job for you this afternoon," Mr Glasse said, trying to suppress a smile. "You'll have to repair that cart."

I examined the damage and when I looked into the cart I saw that the floor did not look too sound. By just prodding I made a hole in the rotten floor boards. We had been extremely lucky that the bull had not stepped through the rotten wood on our journey. The bottom could very easily have fallen out of the cattle cart. It would have been a very funny sight to have the cart drawn by a horse, two men sitting on the bench and the bull walking behind under cover of the wooden box.

It took me two days to rebuild the cart before it was returned to its owner in much better condition than when we had borrowed it.

Some time later, Crane and I were trimming the hedgerows in the same meadow. We always carefully collected the trimming for later use in building the bottoms of corn stacks.

When the time came to cart the trimmings to Waterman's End stack yard, Crane asked: "Which horse we got to have?"

"Let's not have the black one," I replied. "Daisy is a bit fresh." Nobody ever wanted to use this horse, but you could not have said a more challenging thing to Crane.

"We'll use Daisy," Crane commanded stubbornly.

We got the black horse hitched up and went to Daniel's Mead. I got off to open the gate.

"You just be careful how you come in here," I called to Crane. "Let me lead her in."

No, he wouldn't have that and 'crash', over went one gatepost.

"See what you have done now", I said, exasperated. "You have knocked the gatepost over."

"And I knock the other one over," he retorted, defiantly. "Then they'll both be down." And he did, smashing the gate in the process.

Needless to say, we had to repair them. "That's Crane again," Mr Glasse said. Nobody except Crane would have got away with it. Anybody else would have been sacked for such behaviour.

But Crane was a tough old bugger and was not fazed by anything. Once, when we had stopped at a pub for a pint, somebody pointed to the window and said: "Look, that gang of gypsies is getting ready for a fight."

197

"Oh dear," I said. "Our bicycles are parked just behind them."

Crane looked, downed his beer, wiped the froth of his moustache and walked out into the yard. The gypsy women were shrieking and two of the men were growling at each other, their fists raised ready for a real fisticuffs.

Crane walked over to them. I remained standing in the doorway, feeling somewhat apprehensive. It was not my idea of fun to be drawn into a gypsy fight. Crane hit the first one and sent him sprawling in one direction. Then he turned his attention to the second one and hit him into the other corner.

"Here you are, Fred," he said, calmly handing me my bike. Then he walked back, calmly collecting his own -- right through the middle of a lot of shouting and threatening gypsies.

"They can't fight when they are sober," he said, turning to me. "I'm bloody sure they can't when they are drunk."

When one of Mr Thomas Glasse's daughters got married, both Crane and I got into a bit of self-imposed trouble. We had all been invited to attend the wedding at Little Laver, but Crane was not impressed.

The wedding day clashed with the Puckeridge point-to-point races at Silverleys, Bishops Stortford, which we had hoped to attend. It was shortly after the war and we had been deprived of entertainment. This race meeting was something we had very much looked forward to.

"I am not going to attend that bloody lemonade wedding," Crane said. "They are so damn religious, they won't break their principles. There will not be a single drink in sight. I am going to the races instead. Will you come, Fred?"

I did go along and we had an enjoyable day at the races, but I did feel pretty guilty about it. Elsie had made the wedding dress and my son, Maurice, was blowing the church organ. I am quite sure I was none too popular for having refused the invitation. And with hindsight, I can see that it was not very gracious and that it would have hurt the Glasses.

Mr Glasse was very angry with Crane and me, and it took a long time before he was able to be friendly again. While he eventually forgave us, I do not believe that he ever forgot, and I am sure that only the fact that we were two of the strongest, hardest workers on the farm saved us from dismissal.

For a long time thereafter, whenever something came up he would say: "Why should I consider your feelings. You didn't consider mine."

Many years later, after the Glasse family had moved to Little Laver Grange, Crane and I had been asked to do some repairs to the roof at Little Laver Grange as water was getting through into Mr Glasse's bedroom.

We had just put the ladders up when Mrs Glasse came out of the house.

"Fred, while you two are up there, would it be possible to take that chimney pot off?" she said, pointing at one of the pots. "It's of no use -- only a nuisance as birds choose it as a nest site."

"I don't think so m'am," I replied. "We don't have the proper tackle and that pot is heavy."

Crane had obviously heard Mrs Glasse's request. As she walked back into the house, he plonked past me up the ladder and on to the roof. Next I heard him shout: "Mind your bloody head!" -- and the chimney pot came hurtling past me.

With brute strength, he had wrenched the chimney pot off. It had bounced off the roof, smashing many tiles, before zooming past my head and smashing on the patio.

The chimney pot was off. I had not been killed. But the job of roof repairing which should have taken a few hours, now took several days.

At harvest time, Mrs Glasse would frequently come into the field at four o'clock in the afternoon with a tea basket for her husband and her son, Graham.

This was the first harvest on which we used the new invention, a combine harvester, to harvest the barley. The new machine was pulled by a tractor driven by Master Graham. Crane and I were working with the binder, cutting wheat in an adjacent field. As Mrs Glasse walked past us, she stopped for a moment.

"What do you think of the new combine harvester, Crane?"

"They won't last," Crane replied, with an air of finality.

I didn't comment as I knew Crane would most probably sulk for the rest of the afternoon if I disagreed with him, but I thought: I'll bet you anything that they will -- and that they will get bigger and better.

I remember the arrival, many years ago, of the first motor plough -- later to be called a tractor. The first generation did not do a very good job, but they developed very quickly from then on. I had heard many comments about tractors not lasting and that horse power would always be better. But they were quite clearly wrong and logic dictated that anything which makes the work on the land easier, will be here to stay.

And I can earnestly say that in later years I was often grateful when, at the end of a hard day, I had only to park a tractor or combine harvester, rather than having to clean, feed and stable a horse.

Crane was a terrible womaniser. He did not mind who she was; he chased anything in a skirt. He lived to ninety years old and he never gave up. During one of the last occasions I visited the old fellow, I found the butcher's girl waiting outside his house.

"Please stay with me," she said, "the old bugger chased me round the kitchen table last time I was here."

Once, in earlier years, he had even dared to pinch Elsie's bottom. Oh dear, she was cross. She hit him and to the best of my knowledge, he never tried again.

Chapter 18

I have always marvelled at how well Elsie coped with my Granny, considering that they had absolutely nothing in common. When we were first married, Elsie took over the housekeeping and, to the best of my knowledge, there were no problems over this with Granny. I rather think that Granny was quite pleased to pass these responsibilities over to my wife. As any new housewife might, Elsie bought a whole range of new kitchen equipment -- she did not want to make do with Granny's old things.

Granny was getting to be a rather frail old lady by now, even if she was still very cantankerous on occasions, and she took to just pottering around the house. Or she might sit and listen to our wireless set. She took particular delight in listening to the service from St Martin's in the Fields church. Church had been such a major part of her life and she especially loved the hymn singing.

As it got a little more painful for her arthritic bones to get up and down the stairs, we arranged an extension of the loudspeaker from the downstairs radio set to her room upstairs. There she would sit cosily in front of the fire and enjoy her listening. Often she had her friends visiting and she would call out: "Come on up here. We'll have a chat about old times."

Granny was really no trouble at all.

I do remember with amusement when Elsie made a comment about a particular programme we had been listening to and Granny replied:

"That may 'ave been on your set, but it wasn't on mine."

To her generation, radio was still a bit of a mystery.

Elsie and I had been married for three years, when just after we had taken the breakfast tray up to Granny, we heard a terrific thump upstairs. Our eyes automatically swivelled towards the ceiling and then we both rushed upstairs. Granny was lying on the floor, clutching her leg and moaning with pain.

"Granny, what's the matter? What happened?"

She had apparently been trying to draw the curtains and must have turned awkwardly and fallen.

We called a doctor immediately and he found that Granny had broken a leg. With a plain piece of timber, and using every single pair of socks I owned to soften the wood against her skin, he made a splint for the leg. Meanwhile, he sent for an ambulance.

"Where are you taking me," Granny asked the doctor, anxiously. "I don't want to go to the workhouse." She remembered the days all too well when the old and sick of the parish were sent to the workhouse (or poorhouse) to die.

"You are going to be all right, Granny Perry," he replied, soothingly. "I'm sending you to St Margaret's in Epping. You'll be well taken care of there."

St Margaret's had indeed, until a very few years earlier, been a workhouse, but had since been converted into a big hospital.

The ambulance arrived and Granny was carefully carried down our twisting staircase on a soft stretcher. Neither I nor Elsie were allowed to go with the ambulance as they took her to Epping hospital. To have a relative accompany the patient was not the practice at the time..

"Don't worry. I'll be all right, met," Granny said to me, just before the doors to the ambulance closed.

As the ambulance pulled away, I lent against the kitchen window and cried like a child. To see her being taken away from Perry Cottage like that frightened me. It gave me that horrible shock of realisation that my Granny was eighty-five years old, frail and vulnerable, and that I could not help her. After all, in all my thirty-one years I had not spent a single day without Granny. She had always been there when I got home to Perry Cottage. Even after I was married, each evening when I returned from work, after I had greeted Elsie, I would sprint upstairs to see how Granny was.

Harry Tappin, Elsie's father, having heard of Granny's accident -- an ambulance being called to Perry Cottage would be known around the Green within minutes -- came over in his motor car and ran us to the hospital where Granny's leg had meanwhile been put in plaster.

She seemed quite settled and after a while even cheerful.

"Have you brought ma books, boy?" she asked.

Granny loved her books. Having taught herself to read during the First World War, she was now immensely keen on reading. It gave her great pleasure and she would lose herself in them for hours. I was in the habit of buying her as many books as she could read, particularly romantic stories. Once a week, I would get her a copy of Horner's stories. Even now at eighty-five, Granny had wonderful eyesight and could read easily without her glasses.

Occasionally we would catch a lift, but most of the time Elsie and I would bicycle to Epping hospital to visit Granny. She was making good progress and after three weeks we were very hopeful that she would be home again soon. That is until, completely out of the blue, our policeman arrived early one morning. He walked up just as I was just going down the yard on my way to work.

"I am very sorry, mate, but I have got some bad news for you," he said. "Your grandmother died early this morning."

I could not grasp it at first. "My Granny dead? But she was fine last night? What happened? Are you sure there is not a mistake? She was doing fine!"

The truth slowly sank in when he asked me to come along to Epping hospital to identify Granny's body.

She did not look like Granny. Yes, of course she looked liked Granny -- but at the same time she did not look like her. She looked peaceful. But this was not my Granny. Granny had always 'chastised' me as she called it; but we had never fallen out. She had never been lost for a quick or cutting remark -- and there she was, lying quite still, and not a single word from her. It was very strange. But I knew it was she. She was still wearing the pink and white ribbons which she had plaited into her hair the night before.

Two days later, our policeman called again and told us that there was to be a coroner's inquest into Granny's death. We would have to attend, he told us.

I have little recollection of the proceedings except that I was asked how Granny had fallen out of bed. Had she had bad eyesight? As I have explained, she had the most amazing eyesight and I told the coroner as much.

Next, the doctor from Epping hospital gave evidence. Yes she had made good progress but, he explained, these things are known to happen to elderly patients. A fall like that, at her age, was a tremendous shock to the system. The verdict was that Granny had died of natural causes.

I have never known quite what it all meant or what she actually died of. Apparently she just slipped away in the middle of the night. Today, one would most probably have had an autopsy to establish the cause of death. Heart failure? A stroke? I will never know.

It took me an awfully long time to get over Granny's death. I am sure that even the dogs missed her. Judy was only a little puppy and Granny had always saved her a little from her meals. "Give that to the puppy," she would say.

I have such wonderful memories of Granny. How ever much she chastised me loudly and often angrily, I knew she cared a great deal for me. After all, she was the only person I had during most of my life. I think of Granny with great fondness, even if she had to drag me out of bed at the crack of dawn when I was a little boy.

"Come on, little met, ya got to wash ya'r face," she would say. "Yar's got to go to work."

When I got to be a little older, and a girl I was very fond of in a teenage sort of way called round at Perry Cottage, Granny would say, smiling kindly:

"Come on in, Beatrice. I'll get he. He'll put a record on and you'll have a dance."

"Go here boy. There is somebody here t' see ya," she would say to me. "Move the furniture aside. Make a bit of spearce [space] for dancing."

And in our front room we would have a dance, observed by Granny, who was very proud indeed of the new oil cloth, or linoleum, on which we were twirling around. She would titter away all the time, thoroughly enjoying our dancing. She loved having the house full of music and dancing. From her chair she would call out the next record she wanted us to dance to - - possibly 'Valencia', 'Three o'clock in the morning' or 'My great picador'.

I even gave up the chance to go into the police force, which I at the time had badly wanted to do. The preliminary interviews had been no problem and I had very good recommendations. But I could not take it any further as I would have been sent away, first for training and later to a posting. I just couldn't do it. Granny had not been well at the time and I couldn't possibly have left her to fend for herself.

With hindsight, I have no big regret over not having become a policeman. Yes, I would possibly have been a little better off, but I was happy enough on the land. And anyhow, Granny would always have come first.

Oh dear me! And now Granny was no more. Now that we were a little better off and she could have had a glass of stout any time she wanted it, she could no longer enjoy it. Granny's life had been tough. The last few years, when it had become a little easier for her, had, alas, been much too few.

Uncle George and I went to see Mr Blatch, the undertaker, who we knew well, to arrange the funeral. We knew Arthur Blatch to be the best. He would arrange everything. All we had to do was to contact our relatives.

On the morning of the funeral, 6th August 1936, Granny's body was brought home in the hearse for her final journey to High Laver churchyard. The hearse stopped outside our house, as was customary to show that Perry Cottage had been Granny's home. Mr Blatch slowly and ceremoniously walked towards the waiting family group.

"We are ready to take Mrs Perry to her final resting place," he said, and led the way to the mourning cars.

Mr Blatch was the absolute epitome of an undertaker. He totally looked the part. In his black suit, top hat and boots, it was not just as if he was dressed in these clothes, but as if he had been born in them. He was a jolly good carpenter too, but when he did his job as undertaker, he did it as I have never known anybody before or since. You simply knew that he was sincere. He could not possibly have been anything else. I am quite sure that he carried his face in a bag.

I had attended many funerals prepared by Mr Blatch. Whilst standing in church, possibly slightly impatient for the cortege, I always knew precisely when it was about to arrive. It would be preceded by the 'squeak, squeak' sound of Mr Blatch's boots as this tall, upright man walked up the aisle. In latter years and many funerals later, I rather think that he either wore new boots for each occasion or that he had a special spring fitted to his boots to make them squeak.

PHONE: FYFIELD 34.

_____ Aug 193 6

Mr Excrs of the late of Mrs Sarah Ann Perry

DR. TO ═══ **A. BLATCH,**

SHOEING SMITH,

WHEELWRIGHT, CARPENTER AND UNDERTAKER,

FYFIELD, ONGAR, Ex.

MEMORIALS SUPPLIED

£ . s . d

1936

Aug 8th | To Funeral of the late of Mrs Sarah Ann Perry

Supplying Polished Coffin Complete with Brass Fittings & Delivering same to Epping Infirmary Conveying Body from Epping to High Laver for Burial with Hearse, & 3 Mourning Cars for Funeral, Paying Church Clerk & Gravediggers Fees,

£ 13 4 0

R Blatch

Mr Blatch, however, was not always in such a sombre mood. I have also known him to be the life and soul of the party when he sang in the choir at British Legion festivities. He had another, jovial face when he sang one of his numbers, a very jolly song, in duet with the local doctor. It always struck me as slightly funny -- the doctor and the undertaker singing together.

A lot of people came to say their goodbyes to Granny. There were masses of flowers. After the service we invited everybody to come back to Perry Cottage. It was just as well that it was a lovely summer's day and we could spill over into the garden. The house could not possibly have held that many people.

208

"Did you ever see a funeral with more flowers than at Granny Perry's?" I heard somebody ask Arthur Blatch.

"Yes," he replied sincerely. "I have. I buried a gypsy last week and you could hardly get into the churchyard for flowers."

I can full well believe this as I had experienced a gypsy funeral procession myself. An old gypsy woman had lived just down the road from Waterman's End, by the gravel pit. She had been a stately looking, white-haired elderly woman. When she died, hundreds of gypsies came to pay homage. Apparently, she had been a gypsy queen, and Romanies came from all over Essex.

The night before the funeral, they took her body out of the caravan and put it in a specially prepared and decorated tent. Then they shot her horse and set fire to the caravan. This, one of the gypsies told me later, was done to keep the evil spirits away. The mourners sat very solemnly around the fire all night.

The police had to close off the mile long lane past Waterman's End at both ends. I watched the funeral precession go past Waterman's End house. I have never seen so many people in my life. The slow walk past lasted hours and hours.

It was quite fascinating. But though well turned out in their finery, with their swarthy features they still looked a pretty villainous lot. Even days later, gypsies would still come to visit the caravan site.

Chapter 19

Children had, somehow, not featured high on my list of priorities. Life was fine just as it was and the dogs gave me a lot of pleasure without the work and responsibility of children.

Elsie, however, did not share my feelings on this point. Elsie wanted children.

"I am going to see the doctor and have him check me out," she said in a matter-of-fact voice one day. "I can't make out why I haven't fallen pregnant yet."

I knew jolly well why not and at this point I decided that I had better get on with it, before the good doctor did -- after all, my wife was a lovely looking woman.

Maurice & Margaret Perry

Maurice John Perry was born on the 30th July 1938. I named him after Maurice Nichols, the great England and Essex bowler in the hope that Maurice might become a good player -- but he never took the slightest bit of interest in cricket.

In all other respects, though, he has been a most marvellous son and a constant joy and pride to me.

On the next occasion, Elsie was the

smarter of us. She must have outwitted me. Margaret Ann Perry was born on the 24th March 1940. Today, and for many years now, I have been delighted that Elsie knew best and gave me two wonderful children. From the day they were born, I would not have wanted to be without them and I would have done anything for them. I consider myself a very lucky man indeed. As it happens, they have never needed my help. They have been able to stand readily on their own feet and I have never needed to worry about them.

Nowadays, one hears so often of fathers deserting their children. Even if Elsie and I had ever fallen out -- which we did not -- I could never have left those lovely children of mine.

Maurice, right from the young age of five, was a little worker. He had a certain independence and will about him. He would get on his small bicycle and go up to Waterman's End to help the contractors pick peas. He would be given a bag which he would fill with pods and be paid a few shillings.

When a little older, for a small reward, he would help with tasks in Squire's house and at the age of thirteen he was quite adept at driving a tractor. We would put it in the field for him and he would get on with baling hay or straw. He was not pushed into any of these tasks. He just liked being independent. But Maurice eventually decided, quite rightly, that he did not want to be a farm labourer like his father.

Margaret, right from birth, was as pretty as a picture. She was the most delightful, pretty little blond girl. In her own way, she was equally determined, but she got her way in a more feminine manner.

I recall one morning that Elsie came up to Waterman's End

"I had to take Margaret to school," she said. "I had no choice." You see, everybody else was going to school, including her friend Shirley, and Margaret had decided that at four years of age she should go too. It is just as well that the schoolmaster accepted her, as she would surely have sat in the school porch all day.

She even charmed Squire. She used to run up to him, as fast as her little legs would carry her and give him a kiss -- initially much to his embarrassment.

During working days I now saw very little of Squire, but I would call on him regularly after work or at weekends. I had grown very fond of him over the years and Squire was getting older and was not terribly well. He suffered badly from gout and eventually had to give up his beloved shooting. By this time, my mother had worked for him as housekeeper for a few years. Mrs Allen, Squire's trusted housekeeper of many years, had left to get married. Two new housekeepers followed in rapid succession. The first one lasted only a week because she would have drunk him out of house and home, and the second one drove us all mad as she had got 'religion' with a capital R. She was a born-again Christian. Whilst we were all fairly religious, she took things too far.

"Hallelujah, the golden age is at the gate. Hallelujah," she would invariably say when she saw me.

One day I found Squire in the brewhouse, which was unusual for him.

"What are you doing in here, sir?" I enquired in surprise.

"If somebody does not get rid of that bloody woman, I shall go mad," he replied. "I am trying to boil an egg for myself. Can't stand another lecture from her." That, I think, was the only time I ever heard Squire swear. Poor man, he was at his wit's end. After two weeks, the housekeeper was let go.

It was really quite providential that Mother was at home at the time and she was approached to see if she would consider taking the position. Mother, who had been housekeeper in much grander households, accepted.

212

"I will be lowering my standard, but it will suit your Granny," she said. As Granny was getting older, Mother wanted to be nearer home. Old Mrs Lucking had interviewed her and Henry Lucking always chuckled about it and said: "She is the only one who can stare down my mother." Mother often roared with laughter at old Mrs Lucking's antics and she handled her well. Squire told me that it had taken a load off his mind.

"I can sleep peacefully in my bed again knowing that your mother is taking good care of things," he said. Mother insisted on another female servant to assist her, and Mrs Houchin, who was known to Mother, was hired. She was the same age as Mother and twice the size. She was to be the servant -- pure and simple.

Mother had always been a stickler for details and etiquette. She would not have wanted to live in the same house with an unmarried man, even if this man was an elderly, impeccably behaved gentleman like Squire. I am sure she looked after Squire well and I am equally sure that he was a very good employer to her.

I spent many enjoyable hours with Squire. He was getting rather lonely and looked forward to male company. It was during those latter years that I learned to understand him and his family background so much better. In a way, it was very sad that Squire had not married. He would have been a kind husband and it would possibly have saved him from a lot of loneliness. But he had been put off the institution of marriage by his stepmothers.

Even though we never crossed the respective thresholds of our very different backgrounds -- education and upbringing -- we nevertheless became friends. To have crossed those borders would have been unthinkable and neither of us would have wanted it any other way. Squire came from his world and I came from mine.

At one stage, Squire asked if I would help him by writing his cheques. His hands were rather crippled by gout and it was no longer easy for him to write. I thought about it for a while and then I went to talk it over with my Uncle George.

Henry Lucking, 1875 - 1935, and Uncle George, 1883 - 1977 in Squire's rose garden - circa 1910

My mind was a little troubled by the request for whilst I knew that I would never cheat Squire, I also knew that it was

214

very likely that he was being cheated. A few times I had heard him make comments like: "I thought that I had settled the bill with the wine merchant last week. Oh well, he has sent a bill in again, so I must be wrong." And he would settle it again. I am quite sure that some unscrupulous tradesmen had got wind of the fact that Squire did not keep very careful accounts. Particularly not after a few glasses of his favourite port.

Uncle George advised me against taking on the task. "That's not our place," he suggested. "That is a responsibility you cannot take." I agreed with him. I was too worried that if ever anything was ever found to be remiss in Squire's estate, if I handled his financial affairs in any way, the finger would first be pointed at me. A mere labourer would be an easy target. Much as I wanted to help Squire, however, it had to be within the bounds of my capabilities and I would not have been able to afford a lawyer to defend myself. It was better that I should not be involved.

I asked Squire to obtain more professional help with his financial tasks than I could offer. He unfortunately did not do so, but just muddled on. Over the years, I have often thought about it and wondered if my decision was the right one as I am sure he was diddled on more than one occasion.

Chapter 20

The great depression in farming basically lasted until the start of the Second World War in 1939. From that day on, worries for the farmers were over. One could see the difference within a week or two of the war starting. Farmers could borrow all the money they wanted. New, badly needed equipment appeared almost overnight and even farm labourers had their wages increased by five shillings.

Many grants were available to farmers. They could do no wrong -- just plough up a bit of meadow land and a grant would be coming their way.

As an agricultural worker, I was classified as essential for work on the land and was unable to join the forces. Somehow, at first, during the period which is now known as the 'phoney war', our souls were not greatly stirred. Gas masks were issued and rationing became commonplace. Prime Minister Neville Chamberlain had lulled us into a false sense of security and during the early months of the war the real fighting seemed remote.

Churchill made a patriotic appeal for local defence volunteers, which later became known as the Home Guard. Since I was not able to join the army, I joined the volunteer force as soon as possible. Moreton, an adjoining village, was the first section of our local Home Guard to be formed and it was led by Mr E. W. Bovill, then in residence at Little Laver Hall. It was an obvious choice as he had fought in the First World War. The Matching branch was only formed later and by then I was very involved with Moreton. And there I stayed throughout the war.

By the middle of 1940, the war had hotted up and we were absolutely convinced that Hitler's forces would be landing on our shores at any time. I am still not quite sure why he did not, most probably because of pure bluff by Churchill, who had taken over as Prime Minister. In the early days of the war, we would have been a pushover. We had pitchforks and the odd shotgun to defend the country. Our local defence forces initially were in pretty poor shape, but matters improved considerably later in the war and we were well equipped. I guess the pre-war Prime Ministers Stanley Baldwin and Chamberlain had a lot to answer for Britain being quite so unprepared for war. They should have listened to Winston Churchill. He had been warning about the German military preparations for years.

Mr Bovill, or now Captain Bovill, made plans to defend Moreton in the event of the German invasion. Our stronghold was the bakery. The east facing wall had peep holes made to allow us to observe the road coming from Scotts Farm, past Nether Hall, to Moreton, and to stick our shotguns through.

We were issued with bags of flour, a valued and rationed commodity, for the express purpose that we would throw these bags of flour at the German tanks and thus confuse them or obstruct their view.

Quite what we would have done with the 'confused' German fighting force once we had brought them to a grinding halt, I am not quite sure. Nor could Mr Bovill answer my tongue-in-cheek question as to how he could be so certain that the Germans would be coming down that particular road, rather than any of the others that meet at Moreton. There were no holes in the bakery wall facing any other road.

It did not seem altogether plausible to me that, if the Jerry's tanks made it as far as Moreton, they could be stopped by bags of flour, pitchforks and a few shotguns. After all they had overrun Poland in three weeks and we were trying to stop them with 'flour power'. Possibly it was unkind of me to raise these points. After all, Mr Bovill was trying to do his best, and preventing a tank driver from seeing out of his small viewing slit was not such a bad start.

Over the war years, things improved and we received better training and weapons. And we must not forget that it was a pretty terrifying war. There were air raids more or less every night. Essex was very much in the front line and we had several airfields around us. I became the staff sergeant of the Moreton section and it was our job to help in the defence of North Wield airfield. And while I have many amusing stores to tell which would have made good material for an episode of 'Dad's Army', it was also deadly serious and, at most times, very hard.

We worked on the land from daybreak -- remember we had double British summer time -- until dark to help feed a nation which had difficulty in importing food and yet had to feed the population. After work, I would go home to change into my uniform and cycle the three miles to Moreton for night duty.

Often I had to cycle around for miles and read the King's regulations to the various volunteers. Only if they had been read the King's regulations before they went on duty, were they eligible for compensation if anything happened to them in the line of duty. We were a true volunteer force, but we did receive cycle money -- a pittance of one penny per mile.

We guarded the airfield and patrolled the roads and villages. Often after a night of incendiary bombs having been liberally dropped over the area, the Home Guard and many local people spent the rest of the night putting the fires out.

The Home Guard men were on duty until six o'clock in the morning. One morning, Jack Walden, my neighbour, and I were cycling home together from Little Laver Mill, where we had been on observation duty. Suddenly, we heard the sound of a plane overhead, immediately followed by one, two, three, four, five, six explosions -- the sound gradually getting closer.

We knew that we would have to turn around immediately and investigate. The plane had almost certainly been on a mission to bomb London and jettisoned its bombs en route home. One bomb had fallen near Little Laver rectory. The second one in the rectory garden. The third was within yards of Little Laver Mill, exactly where Jack and I had been standing ten minutes earlier.

A fourth one landed in the field and two more in Brick Kiln woods. Each one left a huge crater and I shudder to think what would have happened to Jack and me if we had not left our observation post at six o'clock precisely. And this dallying had made me late for my usual day's starting time of seven o'clock.

Much of the time we were just plain dead tired. That's why my temper was not at its best when an American soldier tried to mock me. Exhausted and fed up as I was, I had cycled around to put some men on guard duty. I was reading the King's regulations, when I saw an American from a ground crew frolic around and mimic my reading and generally make fun of the Home Guard.

These soldiers were not well liked by us. They did not suffer the shortages we experienced, they had decent uniforms and seemed to lead a very pampered life. Their working day finished at four o'clock in the afternoon when we still had four hours of work ahead of us -- followed by Home Guard duty. Sometimes they would try to taunt us by waving at us, already 'poshed up' for their evening drinking session at the pub. They would unzip their flies trying to show us that they were already wearing the condoms they were anticipating using that evening.

On this particular occasion, I had had enough. My patience snapped, and I turned around and hit the American, sending him sprawling. Before he could get up, an American military police jeep pulled up:

219

" It's all right sergeant," they said. "We saw what happened. We'll take care of him." And with that they dragged the soldier to his feet, piled him into the back of the jeep and drove away.

I do not, however, wish to generalise. Not all Americans stationed locally displayed such antagonistic behaviour. There were many nice ones amongst them and they tried hard to help the locals. Sometimes they would invite the village children to one of their picture shows or hold Christmas parties for them with presents which we could certainly not have afforded ourselves. These were hard times for us, and they were trying to help.

Squire, rather saddened at being too old for active service in the defence of his country, did all he could to help. He had loaned all, bar one, of his shotguns to the Home Guard and he kept one room in the house especially for them. A fire would be kept going at all times and the guards on patrol could pop in to warm themselves up or have a hot drink.

We happened to be dead in the path of German planes and often they would jettison their bombs over our area before they reached the coast on their flight home.

It was very exhausting for me, but it was equally hard for Elsie. Every evening, I had to leave her and the children alone, not quite knowing what the night would bring. As soon as the air raid siren sounded, which was most nights, our dogs, Gerry and Judy, would hide. One would dive under Maurice's cot and the other under Margaret's cot. So much for my brave dogs. As you can imagine, I did not feel too good about leaving my family on their own at night, but think of how much worse it must have been for the chaps at the front, and their families, who knew little of the whereabouts of their menfolk.

The training of the Home Guard was one of the greatest problems we faced. Early on we practised with wooden dummy grenades. Mr Bovill would measure out the practice site by striding along the path counting the yards. At regular intervals, whenever he had counted to a round number, he would bend down and push a wooden marker into the ground. On this occasion, Mr Bovill did not realise that a billy goat had taken an interest and was ambling up behind him. We did try to warn him, but apparently he did not hear. The next time he bent down to place a peg, away went the goat. It timed its charge into Mr Bovill's rear perfectly -- and finished the measurement for him.

Some months later, we used live ammunition, but not all volunteers were cut out for warfare. An instructor from the Essex regiment came to train us. We had a huge sandpit into which we threw the hand grenades under his watchful eye. I recall one trainee being absolutely terrified. He managed to pull the pin, but as the lever jumped in his hand, he dropped the grenade in fright. As quick as a flash, the instructing sergeant picked the live grenade up, shouted for us to take cover, and hurled it into the pit. I am grateful his reaction was so swift and professional or we would all have been killed. A farmer from a neighbouring village was killed in a very similar incident.

I recall another incident which illustrated clearly that not all men were responsible or well trained enough to carry a rifle either.

One night we were called out and, as usual, my neighbour, Jack Walden, and I got onto our bicycles and set off towards Moreton. We had just passed Waterman's End when suddenly one of the Matching Home Guard patrolmen jumped out of the bushes. He nearly knocked me off my bicycle, poked his rifle in my neck and called out: "Halt, who goes there."

"Identification card, Freddie," he lisped.

221

"You want an identification card from me," I asked, incredulously. "You have known me all my life," I shouted. "Take that rifle off my neck, you bloody fool."

Jack Walden grabbed his arm, pulled the rifle away and barked at him: "Take your bloody finger off that trigger."

I believe that men like him should never have been issued with a rifle. After all, guns are not toys -- they kill. This man had indeed known me all his life and I have told you about him before: he was the fellow, Stanley Owers, who used to drive us to away cricket matches in his coal van.

Jack and I got back on our bicycles and continued down the road when, lo and behold, I had a puncture.

"Damn it," I cursed. "This is not going to be my night. I have a flat and no puncture repair kit with me."

"We'll soon see to that," Jack said, and took his wallet out of his pocket. As I looked on puzzled, he took a penny stamp from his wallet, licked it thoroughly and stuck over the puncture.

To my amazement, the tyre held air and the penny stamp stayed on the tyre for several weeks.

Another dangerous occupation was practising with what were called SIP bombs. These were bottles of about half a pint in size, filled with a thick yellow liquid. The bottles were stuck on a stick in our rifles. The rifle shot these projectiles several hundred yards at our chosen target. For the target, Mr Bovill had selected a gnarled old tree in Park Wood behind Little Laver Hall. Most of us missed the target, but one chap hit it dead on. The projectile hit a large hole in the tree trunk -- and set it alight. We tried to douse the fire but the old tree blazed away. There we were, nearly at nightfall when blackout had to be rigorously enforced, with Matching airfield just across the field. We had to drag a hosepipe over from the hall and took it in shifts to douse the tree all night.

Occasionally some of us were seconded, for a couple of weeks at a time, to the division in Bradwell-on-Sea, on the Thames estuary, to help defend the sea wall. There were miles and miles of poorly protected coastline and it was of great concern to us.

After two or three years in the Home Guard, I was invited to participate in officer training courses in Frinton-on-Sea. We were billeted at the Majestic hotel and were very well looked after. We were served rather good food, better than Elsie could provide on our rationing. I recall us trainees sitting over coffee after lunch when the shout 'on parade' was heard. I was sitting with a very nice chap, but a particularly big man. He held the dainty coffee cup with his thumb and index finger, just as if he had been some 'toff' officer. As he was trying to set his cup down to rush out on parade, he found that his thumb was firmly stuck in the cup handle. "What can I do, Fred? he asked, holding the cup up with his thumb. I had to laugh. It looked so ridiculous, his great big hand with a little coffee cup stuck on his thumb. I took his hand and knocked it against the edge of the table and the cup came clean away from the handle. He went out on parade with the cup handle still around his thumb.

This chap could make me laugh very easily. Whenever we had to black out our faces for night duty, this great big man would look like a grotesque big giant. I once said to him; "If you were to look over the sea wall with that black, smudgy face during an invasion, the Germans would turn right back."

"You look at yourself, mate," was his reply. "I think you might look better yourself without boot polish."

The officer courses were very enjoyable. I was always keen to learn more and to absorb new things. But to become an officer? No, that was out of the question. I wanted to stay with my friends, to remain one of them. I worked with them, lived in the same village, and I did not want to antagonise anybody by being promoted over their heads, particularly over the heads of men who had actually seen active service in the First World War.

Fortunately, there was never any need to put the military effectiveness of the Home Guard to the test, and during the last period of the war, when there was no real threat of a German invasion any longer, I enjoyed the camaraderie of it.

This war, despite the fact that it lasted two years longer than the First World War, was lighter on casualties. Given the horrid circumstances, Churchill had done a very fine job for t he British nation and the world -- he defeated Nazism. Sixty thousand civilians were killed on the home front in German air raids and a total of 270,000 servicemen and women lost their lives but -- and I think this was a major achievement under Churchill's leadership -- ninety-five per cent of the armed s ervices returned home. Britain had, however, sacrificed her wealth and in effect her empire by winning this war, and, with hindsight, I am not quite sure who the true winners were. We got the prestige, but the big economic powers in today's world are Germany and Japan.

I wish we had a Churchill to get us out of the political mess we are in now. None of today's politicians seems any good. What a mess they have made of things for their own 'sleazy' reasons! Care about the country? Pah! And that applies to most of them. Sometimes I get so angry that I do wish they would stop calling each other 'The Right Honourable Gentleman' (or 'Lady'). There seem to be only a few honourable ones amongst them.

Towards the end of the war, Squire had sold the farm, the buildings and houses to his tenant, Mr Glasse. As a result of this transaction, the Glasse family moved to Little Laver Grange, and Squire, with his entourage of my mother as housekeeper and Mrs Houchin as servant, moved to Waterman's End.

Squire's greatest sadness in moving was having to leave his beautiful rose garden behind. He had always been a great rose expert and enthusiast. He had belonged to the National Rose Society and was a Fellow of the Royal Horticultural Society. The garden at Little Laver Grange had contained more than one thousand roses.

Most evenings, I would call on Squire at Waterman's End and sit with him for a while in his study. Sometimes, I took one or two of the Italian prisoners of war who were working on Little Laver Grange. They were very nice men and Squire enjoyed their visits. He would bring out books about Italy and tell them of journeys to their country which he had made in younger years.

VE day, celebrating the end of the war, was one of the last days Squire actually ventured out of the house. Supported by his shooting stick, he walked from Waterman's End to the cricket pavilion on Matching Green to listen to the speeches and see the bonfire.

Squire had recently been very poorly and the doctor had told mother: "He will not get any better. Does he have any family? You might let them know."

Mrs Charlotte Douglas, Squire's sister, duly arrived -- and stayed. She was the widow of a naval captain who had been a governor of the Isle of Wight under Queen Victoria. Now she lived in Weymouth and Mother could not stand her. Mrs Douglas was pompous, snobbish and, worst of all in Mother's eyes, she wandered around the house constantly with a drink in her hand. I quite liked her, but she must have drunk Squire's cellar dry during his last few months.

225

At three o'clock in the morning one day towards the end of September 1945, my mother came to Perry Cottage. We had not heard her come in and there she stood at the end of my bed trying to wake me.

"Fred, Squire has just died. Will you come up and see to him," she asked.

I was pleased that she had called me. He would not have liked the women in the house, my mother, Mrs Houchin or Mrs Douglas, to have taken care of him. I got dressed and walked up to Waterman's End. I washed and dressed the body in readiness for Mr Blatch, the undertaker. Squire would have appreciated that we gave him the dignity in death of being prepared by his faithful servant and friend.

A short while later, the doctor arrived to issue the death certificate.

"Well Fred," he said, throwing a last glance at Squire, "even in death he looks courtly."

Mr Blatch arrived at what was considered the right hour, dusk, to measure Squire for the coffin.

Squire was laid out in the open coffin at Waterman's End, and over the next few days many people came to pay their respects. He had been a tremendously respected man and in death he was treated almost like royalty. He had been the last absolute Squire of the parish.

Squire's other sister, Mrs Van der Gucht, insisted that I ride in the car leading the mourners, together with Mrs Douglas. She knew of my special relationship with her brother. "It's got to be Fred," she said. "He has done for him and been more of a friend to him than anybody else." Everybody told me what a great honour it was to be asked to lead the mourners. I did not feel quite like that -- honoured. I was not one bit embarrassed at accepting the position. I had been a good friend to him and would probably also mourn for him more than most.

When the funeral procession reached Little Laver churchyard, the coffin was carried up the path and into the church, followed by a solemn looking Mr Blatch in his squeaky boots. The guard of honour was formed by the local police force, headed by the superintendent and his sergeants. Next in line, Squire's fellow magistrates and all the local dignitaries stood to attention. The churchyard was brimming with mourners.

I took Mrs Douglas's arm and, following the coffin, led her past the guard of honour into the church and to our allotted places, accompanied by the sound of the organ.

During the service, many notable persons gave an address expounding Squire's many fine qualities. I recall that the police superintendent, in his dark blue braided uniform, spoke of Squire's scrupulous fairness as a magistrate.

Squire had been a darn good man, the likes of which we are not likely to see again.

He was buried in the style he deserved, in the plot which he himself had chosen -- not in the Meyer family vault, but nearer to Little Laver Grange, right next to the Luckings.

Some weeks later a farm worker approached me and said:

"So, I am talking to a wealthy man today, Fred."

I had no idea what he was talking about until he showed me the local newspaper, which had printed details from Squire's will:

This is the last will of me Herman James Meyer of Little
Laver in the county of Essex, and I hereby revoke all former
wills and testamentary dispositions made by me.

I BEQUEATH the following legacies all free of duty namely:
TO my late Housekeeper Mrs Allen -- Fifty pounds
TO my servant Frederick John Perry who has worked for me
for many years -- One hundred pounds
TO Ellen Eliza Perry, in recognition of her great help in
looking after Mrs Jane Lucking -- Fifty pounds
TO my domestic servant Mrs Houchin -- Twenty pounds
and
TO Albert Clarke of Gosling Hall, Little Laver, who is
stockman to Mr Glasse my Tenant -- Thirty pounds.
Signed and witnessed 12th November 1942.

Bless him, the kind man had left me one hundred
pounds, and my mother fifty pounds in his will. That was a lot
of money in those days and for a farm worker like me it was a
very comfortable feeling to be able to put one hundred pounds
in the bank.

Some years later, quite out of the blue, as I did not even
know that she had died, Mrs Douglas, Squire's sister, also left
me one hundred and fifty pounds in her will.

Chapter 21

Rats, as in Mr Lucking's time, remained a problem and I suspect will always remain a problem on any farm which keeps livestock or stores grain. Recently, I have been told that the country is suffering a rat infestation -- even in the towns. The radio informs me that apparently rats now outnumber humans in Britain.

To prevent any potential problem, Mr Glasse had a contract with the local rat catcher, Mr Joby, to call four times a year.

On this occasion, Joby came to Waterman's End to see if his services were needed. Whilst he was walking around the farm buildings on his inspection tour, he started to curse and swear. Something was clearly wrong with his boot, and his foot was hurting. He limped back to his van, opened the small doors at the back and plonked himself on the floor of the vehicle to deal with his sore foot.

"What do you think you are doing? What's wrong?" Mr Glasse asked. He was a very devout Christian and did not approve of swearing.

Joby explained with a more few more choice swear words precisely what his problem was -- that of a bloody sore foot.

"Where do you think your soul will go if you carry on like that?" Mr Glasse said.

"Over that bloody roof with the uppers if I can get the bloody thing off my foot," Old Joby said. He pulled the offending brown boot off and hurled it over the roof of a farm building where it hit the roof tiles with a clatter.

Then he put on the pair of slippers which he usually kept for entering houses where there might be a rat problem.

Old Joby was quite a character. He was rough and ready, and as big as a barn. Apparently, during his entire married life, he only ever addressed his wife as Woman, while she addressed him as Man.

When Joby was coming towards the end of his days, he said to his wife: "Woman, I'm dying."

"Man, I know y'ar, and I'll bu'n ya," his wife replied, confirming that she would comply with his wishes and have him cremated.

Another local, Walter, who came to the farm for some occasional work, amused me. On one occasion, we had had a lot of snow and we were in Waterman's End yard mixing cattle food. It was Walter's job to cart the chaff away. As usual he was ranting and complaining about Mr Glasse.

"He's no farmer. You ma'k ma word. He's no farmer and never will be. Not like old Lucking," he said.

As I saw Mr Glasse walking into the yard, I nudged Walter to make him aware of the governor's approach.

You could have bowled me over when I abruptly heard Walter's thin and squeaky voice break into song, while suddenly looking very busy:

"What a friend we have in Jesus,
What a grief and pain to bear,
All because we do not carry
Everything to God in prayer."

"Good morning, sir," he said turning towards Mr Glasse. Walter, of course, knew that Mr Glasse was a strict 'chapel' man and was out to earn a few brownie points.

One of the nice things about our farm was that the work was very varied. It was a mixed farm: apart from growing crops, we farmed sheep, pigs and cattle. On a wet day, when we were unable to get on the land, we labourers would help Albert Clarke, the stockman. Clarke was a darn good stockman who had worked at the farm for as long as I can remember. He was already a very experienced stockman when, as a little boy, I started working for Squire and Lucking. He was short and stocky with a stiff waxed moustache. What he lacked in height, he made up for by strutting his chest out and puffing through his moustache. To be a stockman was an important position and it showed in his dress: a beetle tailed jacket, gaiters and a bowler hat.

In Squire's time, we knew that if Clarke went to see him, either somebody would be fired, or he had spotted somebody poaching.

I always got on fine with him, but he could be a very difficult blighter. By the time of the following incident, Clarke had become a crusty, foul-tempered old man. Yet sometimes we threw caution to the wind and mischievously dared to play a joke on him.

Clarke lived in Gosling Hall, one of the houses belonging to the farm. It was just along the road from Little Laver Grange, and we always kept some cattle in the Gosling Hall barn. Consequently, whenever Clarke went home for lunch, he would take a wheelbarrow full of cattle feed with him. One day, when I saw his barrow parked outside the house, I took a piece of string about fifty yards long, which the thatcher working on the barn had left behind. I tied it to one leg of the barrow and an old bottle to the other end.

As Clarke pushed his barrow back after lunch, he met Mr Thomas Glasse in the yard.

"What are you doing, Clarke?" Mr Glasse asked. "Bringing the empties back?"

231

Clarke turned round, saw the bottle clattering behind him and swore furiously. He gathered in the string, cursing all the while, grabbed the bottle and flung it as far into the field as he could. Then he stormed back and hurled abuse at the thatcher, who obviously knew nothing about it. I don't think he ever suspected me.

Clarke later fell victim to another bit of mischief, when one day Master Graham and I were unloading bales of straw from a cart and carrying them to the big open cowshed. Albert Clarke was waiting in the entrance to receive them. He took one bale, set it down and bent over to cut the string around the straw. Master Graham and I looked at each other as we noticed Clarke's watch poking out of his pocket and its loose chain dangling almost to the floor.

"It would be very easy for it to fall out," Master Graham said, reaching out to the chain.

At that very moment, Clarke, who had not heard him, lifted the bale, and swearing at the cows to get out of his way, moved off into the shed -- leaving Master Graham holding the watch. I shall never forget the look of consternation on his face as he first looked at the watch, at Clarke's back disappearing into the shed, and then at me.

"Quickly," I urged him. "Put it in your pocket."

Master Graham, baffled at having finished up holding the watch, swiftly put it in his pocket. Clarke had a fierce temper and Master Graham knew that he would not think it at all funny that somebody had taken his watch. Even if it had been from the best of motives, as it indeed had, Clarke would not have believed it.

"Don't worry, we'll do something about it presently," I reassured Master Graham. "He'll miss it by lunch time and we'll help him look for it. We can 'find' it and give it back to him."

Just as I had anticipated, by lunch time Albert Clarke came to us muttering and cursing, all in the same breath: "I have lost my watch. You haven't seen it, have you?"

"We'll help you look for it, Clarke," I volunteered.

We pretended to make a very thorough search and after a good while Master Graham spoke up while scratching around in the straw on the shed floor: "Is this it, Clarke?"

"Thank you, young sir," Clarke said, looking extremely pleased. "That was most kind of you to spend your lunch hour looking for my watch."

Master Graham was relieved that this episode was over. He had got into it by accident, but I could see that it had left him feeling thoroughly uncomfortable. I am sure the watch had been burning a hole in his pocket.

During the course of the afternoon, Clarke's daughter came into the yard and handed her father a packet. Evidently, Clarke had asked her to bring it round. He strutted over to Master Graham, looking very important and making sure that all the men in the yard were taking notice.

"Here you are, young sir," he said, earnestly. "I shan't forget your kindness in a hurry." And he handed him the parcel which contained two packets of twenty Players cigarettes.

I was tickled to death, but Master Graham looked ashen. He was mortified, but I nudged him to accept the gift.

"Go on, take them," I whispered. "Don't tell him. He'll kill us if he finds out."

Clarke stalked off proudly, feeling six feet tall, having done the right thing in rewarding honesty.

"What shall I do with them?" Master Graham asked me, with a look of utter astonishment and despair on his face. He had had a very strict and religious upbringing and this deception went totally against the grain.

"Smoke them," I said.

233

"Will you have some?" he asked.

"Gladly," I replied. "Let's enjoy them. It was good fun and Clarke will be pleased for days with his grand gesture."

I am quite sure that he would, at the very least, have taken a pitchfork to us if he had known the truth.

Clarke worked until he was in his eighties. He lived to be ninety-seven and was buried at Little Laver. On the day of his funeral, Master Graham and I were standing together in the church awaiting the arrival of the coffin. We could not help but smile when we heard the 'squeak, squeak' of Mr Blatch's boots. As usual, he wore his long, lantern-jawed face, which grew persistently longer and graver during the service.

Mr Blatch was assisted by his helper and gravedigger, Charlie Bird.

Charlie had almost scared a chap to death when he was digging Clarke's grave. He had wanted to get the job over and done with and had worked late into the previous evening. It was a bright night and he could see sufficiently well to carry on digging. But he also wanted to finish up early enough to be able to enjoy a pint at the pub before it closed.

Hence, as he heard somebody walking along the road, he stuck his bald head out of the grave and shouted:

"What's the time, mate?"

"Still don't know," he told me later. "Didn't see his arse for dust."

My mother died, aged ninety-one, a few months before my sixty-fifth birthday in 1970. Perhaps because her death brought it home to me, yet again, that the clock was ticking away, I decided to retire at sixty-five.

Graham Glasse had taken over the running of the farm from his father many years earlier, and I had enjoyed working for him. He had been a good employer and I would miss him.

234

We had shared many a problem and laughed at many things together. Like the event, which I remember with great amusement, when he had been driving the combine harvester and I the tractor and cart carrying the corn back to the yard.

As was usual, the combine went up and down the field harvesting and Master Graham would signal for me to drive over as soon as the harvester's grain chamber was full. I would pull alongside and we would drive along in tandem while the harvester spewed the grain into the cart. We had done this so often, over so many years, that we could have done it in our sleep.

On this occasion, however, I had pulled the hand throttle of my little 'Allis Chalmers' to the wrong point and the tractor drove at a slower speed than the combine. As neither Graham Glasse nor I had kept watch, the combine harvester had overtaken the cart and pulled alongside the tractor. I was hit by a huge hailstorm of grain. The grain was all over me and reached up to my midriff.

We couldn't help but burst out laughing, despite the fact that we had wasted grain and would have a lot of additional work. The corn had got simply everywhere. I even had to take my trousers off and shake them out.

Talk about being covered with the fruits of the earth...

My last day at work, a Friday, was a very sad day for me. It had been difficult to say goodbye to the Glasse family and all my mates.

They had asked me if I wanted to work on. Graham Glasse's wife, of whom I was very fond, sought me out especially: "They tell me you are retiring, Fred," she said. "Please give it a lot of thought. The place will not be the same without you."

But I felt that I should retire. After all, I had started work at nine years old, part time, and full time when I was twelve. Surely, I should treat myself to some rest.

The Glasses very kindly gave me a leaving present of one hundred and fifty pounds and I was delighted with the gesture. I went home, and sat down straight away to write them a thank you letter.

The next day, my own man at last, I went to the High Laver Hall shoot as a beater and was asked if I would come and join them again the following Wednesday at Enville's. "That's all right," I thought. "This is the life for me."

When I walked home from Enville's shoot on the Wednesday, a sudden thought hit me: what shall I do until the next shoot the following Saturday? I have nothing to do. Nowhere to go.

I was still feeling a little downhearted when I reached home and found that Graham and Jimmy Glasse were waiting for me.

"Fred," Graham said. "We are starting to harvest the sugar beet tomorrow, and Jimmy says he can't do it without you. Will you come and help out?"

I can't tell you how pleased I was to be asked. I had been in retirement for exactly three days and was overjoyed to be asked to go back to help.

Next morning, I got up and went to work, as I had done all my life. I worked all that season until the sugar beet was in. We generally tried to have it completed by Christmas or, at the latest, early January. This still allowed me to get a few days' shooting in before the season was over. On other days, I would be doing tasks at Little Laver Grange like cutting hedges. After work, I would walk with my dog. Often I was joined by a friend, Len Little. He had also recently retired from working on the land, and I enjoyed his company - particularly his dour sense of humour.

One evening, we were walking across Matching airfield together when a very smart car pulled up beside us.

"I am lost," the driver explained to us in a very posh and loud voice. "Can you tell me where 'such and such' village is?"

"No," Len replied, as it was a place we had never heard of.

"Do you know where the 'such and such' road is," the driver persisted, impatiently.

"No," Len said, shaking his head.

"Don't you know anything?" the driver demanded loudly and indignantly. He evidently felt offended by Len's monosyllabic answers.

"Yes," Len replied. "I know where I am -- and you don't. Do you?"

Early the following spring, Master Graham came to see me at Perry Cottage, as he had done on many other occasions. Dear old Graham Glasse. He was such a smashing chap and a good friend to me.

"Fred, will you come to Little Laver Grange with me," he said. "I have a new piece of equipment I want to show you."

When we arrived at the farm, he took me into the barn.

"Come and have a look, Fred," he said. "I want to show you this new drill."

He had bought a wonderful new 'Webb' drill and he was clearly very excited about it. While he was explaining it to me, I suddenly felt very queer. It was almost as if somebody had kicked me in the stomach. I felt very unwell. The birds were twittering in the barn and even this, which I would normally have taken pleasure in, suddenly seemed like a terrible noise. Everything was coming in on me.

For whatever reason, the drill had triggered it off. The dreadful feeling and realisation that I would not be there to use this wonderful new drill. I had gone into retirement and the drilling of the new crops, which for so many years had been my job, would be done by somebody else.

I ran out of the barn. I could not possibly stay any longer. The horrible feeling would not leave me. I just could not shake it off. I felt physically sick and I went home immediately.

For days the horrible low and depressed feeling persisted, and eventually I went to see the doctor. He gave me a thorough examination.

"You are physically in wonderful shape. But we will have to give you something to steady your nerves," he explained.

"I am afraid you seem to have suffered a nervous breakdown," he continued. "I'll prescribe you some tranquillisers. It is hardly surprising, having worked all your life, that retirement might not be right for you. Why don't you see if you can do a little work again? A strong man like you will not have any difficulty in finding a little work to keep you busy."

The tablets helped a little, but the cure arrived in the shape of Graham Glasse.

"Fred, will you come and do the drilling for us?" he asked. "Nobody does it better than you. Please help us out."

I was so ecstatic I could have danced around the room. A huge weight had been lifted off my shoulders. I could have hugged him.

"Of course I'll do it," I almost shouted. "I am so pleased you have asked me. If need be, I would do it for nothing."

Graham Glasse, of course, did not allow me to work without payment. It would have been totally out of character for him to take advantage of anybody, and as soon I arrived at Little Laver Grange he telephoned to find out how much I was allowed to earn without affecting my pension. The tax authorities in those years allowed me to earn seven pounds and ten shillings, and somehow Master Graham managed to spread this over the year so I did not have to rejoin the brigade of tax payers.

I worked for another eleven happy years for the Glasses. First on the land, and in the last few years I helped in the garden. I only retired finally when they moved out of the area.

When I came home one evening, Graham Glasse was waiting for me.

"Fred, I want to tell you before you hear it from anybody else," he said. "We are going to leave the area. We are moving to Suffolk."

I was sad to see them go. I had worked for them for forty-six years, first when they were tenant farmers, then as owners and had grown very fond of them. They had been marvellous employers and friends, but by this time I was also finally ready to retire.

I watched the 'For Sale' signs go up and eventually come down. Waterman's End was sold; Hull Green was sold; Little Laver Grange and the land was sold.

I overheard somebody say: "The new people will have a hard time keeping Fred off their land."

But they were wrong. I was just happy to walk along the roads and paths I had known all my life, accompanied by my old dog, Shep. I was quite content. Retirement wasn't bad at all now.

Chapter 22

At the time I did not realize that retirement was to hold another treat in store for me -- Drammie.

This story would most probably never have been written but for my getting to know Drammie. She was really named Lady McDram, but I have always called her just Drammie.

When she was born in 1983, I was already seventy-eight years old, but I can sincerely say that the age difference has never been a problem. In fact, it simply never came up -- Drammie and I understood each other from the word go.

Not that I knew her right from birth. After my retirement and the Glasses having moved away, new people had moved into Waterman's End. My wife Elsie had agreed to work in the house for them. She told me on several occasions that the new people were very nice. Nevertheless, I preferred to stay clear of the place. Everything had changed so much: Henry Lucking gone, Squire gone and now the Glasses also gone. Also, I still had the comment 'they'll have a hard time keeping Fred off their land' ringing in my ears. I had no heart for getting involved with the newcomers.

"Why should I want to know them?" I asked Elsie. "And anyhow, they have moved here from London. What do they know about Waterman's End?"

They had asked me often enough to stop by. They had most probably heard of my having worked there all my life, but I just did not want to know.

Drammie was born very shortly after the arrival of the newcomers. But as Elsie will tell you, I have never liked 'little one'. The new owners of Waterman's End did ask me to come and take a look at the 'little one'.

Though I wasn't rude to them, I was curt, albeit within the borders of politeness. I took evasive action by walking across the fields, rather than go down the lane in front of Waterman's End. Walking in the countryside is how I spent most of my time. I love the land and the countryside around us is just beautiful.

But, when my lovely old dog, Shep, died, walking along the lanes was somewhat more lonely.

For lack of anything else to do and being a bit bored I called on Elsie at Waterman's End -- just for a chat. While we were standing by the back door talking, Elsie suddenly said in her voice tolerating no argument:

"You have nothing better to do, why don't you take out the 'little one' for a walk down the lane? It'll get her out from under my feet."

This was not exactly why I had called, but grudgingly I took her along with me. By the time we had reached the end of the lane, I had found that even walking out with a 'little one' was better than walking alone. She was company; she was somebody to talk to.

Next day, I called for her again and before I knew what happened, she had crept into my heart. One might say this was the start of a love affair between the very young and the very old. Drammie and I became inseparable.

I called for her every day -- such marvellous company, interested in everything around her. Her little face, with her wonderfully expressive, brown eyes would look up at me with insatiable curiosity and she was such a good listener.

I told her about my starting to work in the field right next to her house. And how, as a little boy of nine, I had worked for Henry Lucking at Waterman's End, chopping the firewood, carrying the heavy coal scuttles into the house, polishing boots and emptying the rubbish pails. In fact, I did anything which might have brought in an extra few pennies to help feed us. I can still see Henry Lucking quite clearly in my mind's eye every time I step through the door into the kitchen at Waterman's End.

Right there by the back door, was the sink where he washed the hens' eggs. I will never forget those huge hands awkwardly trying to handle the eggs. Lucking was always subdued at home, under the watchful eye of his wife, but out on the farm with the men, he was a bundle of fun, always ready to play a prank on somebody.

Waterman's End also holds so many memories of Squire for me. He spent the last year of his life, and eventually, died there.

I told Drammie of the many hours after a hard day's work that I spent in Squire's study, chatting or just keeping him company. He was such a lonely man towards the end of his life -- I do wish he had married and had a family.

Squire had started life a very wealthy man and I do not think that there was a great deal left when he died. Possibly his liking for a glass of good port may, over the years, have exacerbated some poor business judgements. I was saddened to see some years later, that even his last will and testament was witnessed by a wine merchant and his wife.

Eventually, through Drammie, I got to know the new people at Waterman's End. They were nothing like I had envisaged in my prejudices. Possibly some newcomers are all right.

I often think of the various, previous, occupiers of Waterman's End during my lifetime. Lucking? I wonder what the newcomers would have made of Lucking? Squire, I think, would have liked the new people.

They most probably would have dined together and I am sure the governor would have enjoyed Squire's shooting parties. He seems to be just as much of a stickler for shooting etiquette as Squire was. I consider myself lucky to have made this new friend. I have never known a nicer gentleman -- one could put him in a bit of sackcloth and he would still look the perfect gent.

But it was largely the lovely little Drammie that pulled me back to Waterman's End. I would call for her at eleven o'clock each morning and weather permitting we would set off on our walks. If it was foul, we would just go back to Perry Cottage and amuse ourselves there.

And I still remember one terrible day, a damp morning, when Drammie and I were walking back from Waterman's End to Perry Cottage. We were just passing the school when some of the older children called to her from the schoolyard. As quick as her stubby little legs would carry her, she ran across the road to join them. It still sends shivers down my spine to think about it. A car, driving much too fast, appeared out of nowhere and -- thump -- I heard it hit her. She was thrown onto the grass verge. I ran across to her envisaging the worst. The driver, believe it or not, had not even stopped, but I have been told that this it quite common nowadays. Margaret, my daughter, quickly went for help. Fortunately, Drammie did not seem to be badly injured. She was examined and X-rayed, and I am pleased to say that she was only bruised.

My poor little mite spent a couple of very uncomfortable days. I felt terribly responsible: Had I not kept close enough eye on her? Thereafter, I never allowed her to come to the Green without holding her very close. This is not to say that over the years she did not sometimes make her own way to Perry Cottage when she felt like it. We received many a call from Waterman's End to say that Drammie was 'AWOL' from the garden. But I had been very insistent with her and she was a good girl. She invariably came across the meadow at the back of Perry Cottage, avoiding the road.

Sometimes, when the fancy took us, we would visit some of my friends. Old Peter Peacock, for example, of whom you have heard me speak before. We would invariably find him in his garden. He kept a beautiful garden. People would stop and look over the hedge to admire it.

"Hello, Peter," I would call out to him when we got to his gate. "What are you doing in the garden in this weather. Too cold for us. Let's go and sit by your fire."

If Drammie had got distracted and had not gone straight up to greet Uncle Peter, he would scan the garden with his rheumy eyes:

"Where is the little one?" he would ask. It was his first concern that Drammie had come along. His eyesight was getting rather poor and he might not have spotted her immediately. Every week, he would walk up to the village shop to buy a bottle of whisky for himself and, without fail, a packet of Smarties for Drammie.

Peter's house stands just off the Green, around the corner from the post office, in Potash road. It is the very same house the policeman lived in who came to search for the bu'rds which had been hidden under Granny's skirts.

But for the past seventy-five years Peter has lived here. The house has a tiny little parlour. We would all pile in there and Drammie would cuddle up while Peter and I had a good old natter. Or we would chat away while Peter cooked his lunch. It has always amazed me how such a small man could eat such huge quantities of food. Possibly that is his recipe for a long and healthy life: get up as soon as it is daylight; work in the garden; eat plenty of good home-grown food; and have a tot of whisky at night time.

At first, when Drammie was very young and I took her along, I was a little worried that she would be her boisterous self and a bit disruptive, as she was allowed to be at Perry

Cottage. You see, I had never been very good at being strict with her. I always felt that she had to learn things her own way. But I need not have worried. She was as good as gold -- she was universally popular, and I guess she became very spoilt.

When Drammie was about five years old, she became terribly ill. In the beginning, they tried to keep the truth from me, but I knew it was serious. Later, I learned that it was bone cancer, and thank God it proved treatable. But Drammie had to go to London for treatment quite often. I missed her terribly and was desperately worried. I simply did not believe their assurances that she was going to be all right.

But she did get better, I am delighted to say, but was being treated with steroids. I remember that made her ravenously hungry and she became quite chubby. Everybody got mad with me when I gave her treats. I have never seen, my wife, Elsie quite so cross. She accused me of not being interested in Drammie's welfare. Me? Not interested in her welfare? I, who had agonised day and night over her? Did they not understand that the poor little one was hungry? The least I could do for her was to sneak her a bit of food.

Thank God that she could eventually come off the steroids, even though she never quite regained her elfin figure. But who cared about that? She was well again -- and still my beautiful little Drammie.

Drammie and I spent countless hours on the cricket ground together, on our bench. I call it our bench, because two benches were placed there on instructions of the last owner of Little Laver Hall, Mr Henry Douglas Pennant. He and his family lived there for many years and I regret to say that he died much too young. He was a smashing man with a very nice family -- a great loss to Little Laver and Matching Green.

245

I will never be sure how I deserved it, but Henry Douglas Pennant made a will in 1981 and had left a legacy:

to the Matching Cricket Club the sum of five hundred pounds for the purpose of purchasing a seat or seats for use by cricket spectators in memory of Fred Perry who devoted so much time to the cricket ground and club.

As a result, there are now two beautiful wooden benches right at the edge of the cricket ground. I am certain, when Henry Douglas Pennant made his will he did not anticipate that I would outlive him by so many years. Apparently, they tell me that is bad form to put a plaque on them while I am still alive.

I look forward to seeing Henry Douglas Pennant again when my time comes join them all up there. We'll have that great big tea party in the sky. Who knows, Granny, Lucking and Squire might come and join in. How wonderful it would be to see them all again.

I am already a bit more careful in what I do and say. After all, I am ninety years old now, and the time when I will have to meet my Maker must be coming closer.

But for the moment, I am blissfully happy in this world right now. Instead of sitting on a chicken coop, as I did as a youngster, Drammie and I have spent many enjoyable hours watching cricket from a most comfortable seat.

When she was very young, Drammie was a bit of a nuisance on the cricket ground. If I was umpiring, she would not necessarily always behave as I had told her to. Sometimes, she would get off the bench, run right across the pitch and join me. The ball was not always safe either, for she occasionally wanted to join in. Nobody minded too much, or they considered me too old to be given a hard time over it. Everybody got used to her being with me. Her bit of unruly behaviour on the cricket ground improved as she got older and she also redeemed herself by becoming quite adept at fishing cricket balls out of the pond.

The only days when Drammie could not go with me was when I went shooting or beating, but she would almost invariably be waiting for me when I got back to Perry Cottage. Even though I missed Drammie on those occasions, some of my most enjoyable days in my retirement have been spent at shoots. Matching Hall is still one of my favourites and they make me feel very welcome.

Occasionally, their gamekeeper, Clive Bell, would pick Drammie and me up and take us for a ride across their land to check out the pheasant pens or to look for my old friend Charlie Fox. Oh dear, Drammie enjoyed those outings. She would sit on my lap and look out of the window, fascinated by the countryside around her, and listening to us chatting away about the shooting season.

But all of that was before Drammie went blind. My poor little Drammie, despite all the terrible things she had endured in her young life, she still remained cheerful and loving. Even after her eyesight failed, she still seemed to get a great deal of enjoyment out of life. She was my constant companion for so many a happy year. She had gone everywhere with me. We knew every inch of the lanes and the land around us, and on our walks I had told her the story of my long life many times. She was beautiful. She was wonderful company.

247

I grieved very much when she died. The loss of my Drammie, my beloved Cairn Terrier, hit me very hard. That is not to say that I did not love my previous dogs just as much. I am sure I did, but somehow Drammie was special -- possibly because she came to me so much later in life and I had all the time in the world for her. She shared most of my retirement years. I am ninety years old now and I had been quite sure that I would come to the end of my road before she did -- we have walked a long road together.

Fred Perry in 1994

248

The Perry Family

The Dweller Near A Pear Tree

Copyright ©Angela Busch

George Perry Sawyer
b. 1795, Fyfield
m.
Sarah Wakelin
b. 1795, High Laver
**Married at All Saints Church, High Laver, 1824.
Lived in Perry Cottage, on Matching Green in the
Parish of High Laver, Essex**

Sarah Ann Wakeling
(Granny)
b. 1851 Workhouse, High Laver
Daughter of Eliza Wakeling, Spinster
and William Barnard, Widowed Farmer
of **High Laver Hall Farm (350 acres)**
d. 1936

John James Perry Thatcher
(Grandfather)
b. 1846 Perry Cottage
m.
d. 1913

m. **All Saints Church High Laver 1869**

Children of George Perry Sawyer and Sarah Wakelin

William b. 1824 High Laver	Mary b.1826 Writtle	Elvia b. 1827 High Laver	George b. 1828	James b. 1836 m. Mary Ann Saville 1874 High Laver Church	Charlotte b.1840	Ellen b.1842	John James Perry Thatcher

Children of John James Perry Thatcher and Sarah Ann Wakeling

John James b. 1870 m. Dorcas Ann	William b. 1871 d. 1949 un-married	Sarah Ann b. 1873 d. 1955 m. Jack Ellis	Frederick Charles b. 1875 d. 1943 m. Rose	Lizzie May b. 1878 d. 1943 m. Harry Byford	**Ellen Eliza (Mother)** b. 1878 d. 1970

Children (next generation)

Thomas d. in child-hood	Emily d. in child-hood	George Henry b. 1883 d. 1977 m. Lucy Claydon	Elsie d. Canada m. Charles Brooker	Alice Ruth b.1887 d.1966 m. Charles Blowes	Alfred James d. 1918 1st World War un-married	Jessie May b.1897 d. 1951 William Turner

Perry
1. John
2. Maud
3. Ellen
4. Elisabet *b.1899*
5 Frederick Charles
6. William James *b.1901*
7. Doris Beatrice *b.1904*
8. Mary Theodora *b.1906*
9. Charles Harry *b.1909*
10. Alfred George *b. 1912*
11. Walter Lewis

Ellis
1. William
2. Herbert

Perry
1. Frederick Clifford *b. 1904 d. 1974*

Byford
1. Harold
2. Gladys
3. Victor
4. Lesley
5. Olive
6. Ruby
7. Chubb
8. Marjory

Perry
1. Lawrence
2. Nancy
3. James

Brooker
1. Bartram *b. Canada*
2. William *b. Canada*

Blowes
1. George
2. Albert
3. James
4. John
5. Thomas
6. Reginald
7. Stanley

Turner
1. Reginald
2. Stanley
3. Dorothy
4. Elsie

Frederick John Perry *m.* **Elsie Alice May Tappin**
(The Dweller Near The Pear Tree)
b. 14 Nov. 1905   b. 4 May 1910
Married in Little Laver Church 17 Apr. 1933
d. 5 Dec 1996

Maurice John Perry *b.30.7.1938 m. Iris Jones*

Margaret Ann Perry *b. 24.3.1940 m. Albert Shimmen*

Tracy Jane Perry *b.14.8.1966*

Toni Nicola Perry *b.25.8.1968*

Claire Elisabeth Shimmen *b.12.6.1967*

Andrew James Shimmen *b.29.4. 1970*

The Meyer Family

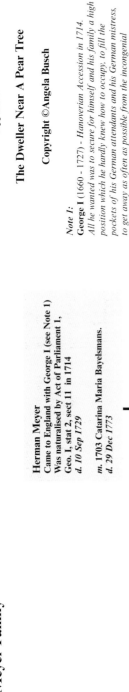

Note 1:

George I (1660 - 1727) - Hanoverian Accession in 1714.
All he wanted was to secure for himself and his family a high position which he hardly knew how to occupy; to fill the pockets of his German attendants and his German mistress; to get away as often as possible from the incongenial islanders, whose language he could hardly speak, and to use the strength of England to obtain the petty advantage for his German principality.

Herman Meyer
Came to England with George I (see Note 1)
Was naturalised by Act of Parliament 1,
Geo. I, stat 2, sect 11 in 1714
d. 10 Sep 1729

m. 1703 Catarina Maria Bayelsmans.
d. 29 Dec 1773

Wendelina b. 16 Jul 1706

Geruth b. 21 Mar 1708

Herman Meyer
Hamburg Merchant
b. 1715
d. 2 Aug 1784 *
Elder of the Dutch Church, Austin Friars
m. 30 Jul 1751, Enfield Church, Co Middlesex
Margaret, b. 1719, d. 8 Oct 1768 *
Daughter of Ebenezer Collier, Sworn Clerk in Chancery,
2 Mar 1710 and his wife Sarah Boddington.
"On the occasion of their marriage all the foreign ships in the Thames displayed their colours."

Anthon
b. 29 Jul 1721
m. Adelheid Vogel
no issue

Christian
b. 26 Jan 1725
d. Jun 1799 in Hackney
m. Hannah Herman in 1767
d. Dec 1799, no iss

Seven sons
and four daughters
died as infants

Catharina
b. 23 Jun 1752
d 2 Jun 1807 *
unmarried
Died at Forty Hall,
Enfield

Herman
b. 1753
d. 1754

James
b. 4 Sep 1755
d. 11 Feb 1826 *
unmarried
Bought his residence, Forty Hall,
Enfield, Co. Middlesex in 1799
for £ 11,940.
His business address
Leadenhall Street

Christian Paul Meyer
b. 20 Jul 1757 - d. 26 Apr 1790
Partner in Firm of Grote & Co.,
Hamburg Merchants
m. Ann Solly, 2 Nov 1789,
Walthamstow, Ex
Daughter of Isaac Solly of Jeffreys
Square,City of London and his wife
Elisabeth Neal
b. 28 Oct 1768, d. 9 Feb 1841 *
The dowager Mrs Meyer bought
Stondon Place, Stondon, Essex from
her husband's cousin -Miss Joanna

Herman
Twin with
Christian Paul
b. 20 Jul 1757
d. 10 May 1832
unmarried

Note 2:

It was largely owing to Christian Paul Meyer's representationsthat his cousin, Miss Joanna Hollingsworth, had purchased Stondon Place. There appears to have been an understanding between her and her cousin, that failing an heir amongst the Hollingworths, the property should eventually come to the Meyers. On Miss Hollingworth's death in 1829, Mrs Ann Meyerbought the estate. By Miss Hollingsworth's will, the money arising from the sale was to be divided into 13 parts. Of these 2/13 were bequeathed to Christian Paul Meyer, 2/13 toHermanMeyer of Forty Hall, Enfield, a twin brother of his father; 2/13 each to Christian Paul Meyer's three daughters, and 1/13 each to his three sons.

Christian Paul Meyer
b. 8 Oct 1790, posthumous
d. 13 Mar 1857
Inherited Forty Hall, Enfield from his uncle James Meyer
Rebuild Little Laver Hall, Essex in 1845

m. 1. Louisa Boddam, 1 Apr 1813, daughter of Rawson Boddam, ex-Governor of Bombay, and of Capels House, Forty Hill, and his wife Eliza Tudor
b. 1794   d. 21 June 1822
m. 2. Mary Walton, 2 Aug 1827, elder daughter of William Walton and his wife Mary Brook - d. 1829
m. 3 Anna Maria Lindigren in Brighton. "She was his daughter's governess." - b. 1793 - d. 25 May 1851
m. 4 Anne Costello - The two youngest children's nurse. "To save any more scandal."

Note 3:

Philip Herman Meyer, in 1844 gave a site for a village school, and at his own expense erected a school building upon it. He was a public-spirited man and his purse was ever open to the needs of the parish. He also bought Stondon House. His widow build at herb own expense a chapel extension, a new vestry and organ chamber as a permanent memorial for her husband. She remarried Col. F. J. Baker in 1874 and for some years lived at Stondon House.
(Source - Stondon Massey, Essex.
by E H L Reeve, M.A.. Rector)

1.
Christian Paul
b. 1 Mar 1814
d. 1832 *

1.
James Meyer of Forty Hall, Enfield
b. 2 May 1815
d. 8 Jun 1894

m. 1. Frances Sarah Solly daughter of Samuel Reynolds Solly and Francis Hammond.
d. 12 Mar 1880

m. 2. Geogina Emma Goldfinch daughter of Sir George Maclean, K.C.B., and Sarah Mary nee Lord, and widow of William Agnew Goldfinch

1.
Louisa Joanna
b. 3 Sep 1816
d. 20 Jul 1843 *

1.
Anne Sophie
b. 4 Apr 1818
d. 28 Feb 1843 *

1.
Philip Herman
b. 6 Mar 1820
d. 14 Nov 1870
Lord of the Manor, Stondon Place, Stondon, Essex.
Inherited the Stondon property from his aunt Ann Meyer (see Note 3)
m. Marianne

1.
Eliza Mary (Lila)
b. 15 Feb 1822
d. 25 Feb 1943
m. 1841 Henry Colinwood Ibbetson

3.
Anna Maria
b. 10 Jan 1833
d. 10 May 1910
m. Thomas Haydon Harrison

3.
Christian Paul *
b. 27 Jul 1835
died as an infant

3.

Herman Paul David Meyer
of The Grange, Little Laver, Essex
b. 15 Nov 1837
d. 23 Apr 1893

m. 1 Constance Martin, 20 Sep 1864 fourth daughter of Philip Stuart Feake Martin
b. 1850, - d. 25 Aug 1873
m. 2 Blanche Martin Sister to Constance Martin
b. 1846 - d. 1877 **
m. 3 Emily Lucy Butler
b. 1842 - d. 1924 **

2.
Katherine Meyer
b. 1852
d. 1889

Mary Colven Meyer
b. 1854
d. 1875

Thomas Lindigren
b. 4 Nov 1865
d. 1946
unmarried

Constance Mary
b. 25 Apr 1867
d. 1949
m 1899
Major Stapylton Robinson, R.A.M.C

Catharine Jane
b. 14 Nov 1868
d. 1950
unmarried

Daniel Haydon
2 Dec 1873
d. 1939
Solicitor
m. 1919 Mary Edith Forster

Frederik Herman
5 Apr 1876
d. 1934
m. 1914 Ethel Mary Hume

1.
Francis Sibyl
Mary
b. 1873
d. 1873 **

1. Squire
**Herman
James Meyer
b. 19 Oct 1868
d. 2 Oct 1945 ***

**Unmarried
Died at
Waterman's End,
Little Laver, Essex**

1.
Blanche Evelyn
b. 27 Jul 1867
d. 9 Sep 1953
m. Michael
van der Gucht

1.
Christian Paul
b. 1866
d. 25 Nov 1893 **
Unmarried
Died in the
Hunting Field,
Little Laver, Essex

1.
Charlotte Constance
Freake
b. 18 Jul 1865
m. Captain Angus
Sholto Douglas, RN
no issue

Angus Douglas
b. 25 May 1910
van der Gucht
Married Alice

Benjamin James
b. 17 Jan 1906
van der Gucht
(alias Tenor Singer
Jan van der
Gucht)

Herman Michael
b. 15 Oct 1903
van der Gucht
went to
Singapore
Married Nancy

Gerald
b. 8 Oct 1900
van der Gucht
Married
No Issue

Marie
b. 12 Mar 1899
van der Gucht
went to
South Africa.

Christine
b. 26 Aug 1897
m. Captain
Dixon
lived in
South Africa

* **Buried in Dutch Church, Austin Friar, London**
** **Buried at Little Laver, Essex**

Appendix III

The Dweller Near A Pear Tree

Copyright ©Angela Busch

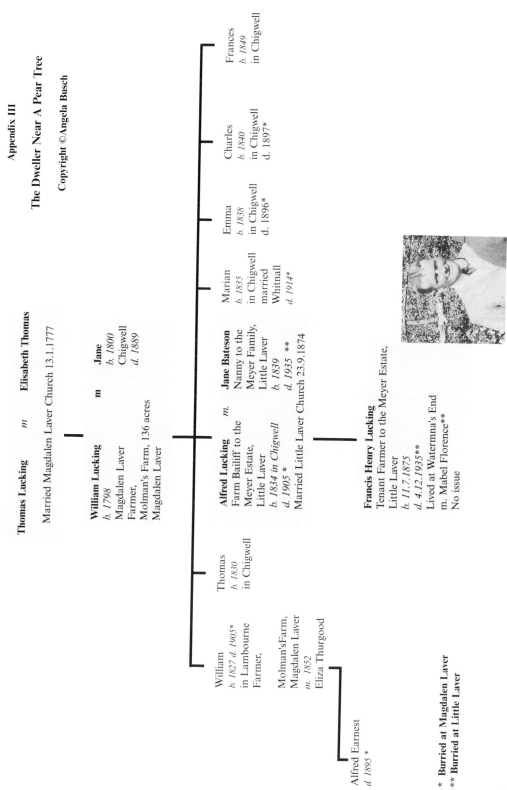

Thomas Lucking *m* **Elisabeth Thomas**

Married Magdalen Laver Church 13.1.1777

William Lucking **m** **Jane**
b. 1798 *b. 1800*
Magdalen Laver Chigwell
Farmer, *d. 1889*
Molman's Farm, 136 acres
Magdalen Laver

Thomas
b. 1830
in Chigwell

Marian Emma Charles Frances
b. 1835 *b. 1838* *b. 1840* *b. 1849*
in Chigwell in Chigwell in Chigwell in Chigwell
married *d. 1896** *d. 1897**
Whitnall
d. 1914*

Alfred Lucking *m.* **Jane Bateson**
Farm Bailiff to the Nanny to the
Meyer Estate, Meyer Family,
Little Laver Little Laver
b. 1834 in Chigwell *b. 1839*
d. 1905 * *d. 1935 ***
Married Little Laver Church 23.9.1874

William
b. 1827 d. 1905*
in Lambourne
Farmer,

Molman'sFarm,
Magdalen Laver
m. 1852
Eliza Thurgood

Francis Henry Lucking
Tenant Farmer to the Meyer Estate,
Little Laver
b. 11.7.1875
d. 4.12.1935**
Lived at Watermna's End
m. Mabel Florence**
No issue

Alfred Earnest
d. 1895 *

* Burried at Magdalen Laver
** Burried at Little Laver